S0-DQZ-277

Flowers from the Bridge

Flowers from the Bridge

MILESTONES TO OVERCOMING GRIEF

RENEE TAFT

**Frontline Communications ● A division of
Youth With A Mission
P.O. Box 55787
Seattle, Washington 98155**

FLOWERS FROM THE BRIDGE

Copyright © 1988 by Renee Taft.

Published by Frontline Communications, a division of Youth With A Mission; P.O. Box 55787; Seattle, Washington 98155.

All rights reserved. No part of this publication may be reproduced in any form (except for brief quotations in reviews) without the written permission of the publisher.

All scriptural references are quoted from the Revised Standard Version of the Bible, unless otherwise noted.

Scripture quotations marked KJV are from the Holy Bible, King James Version.

ISBN 0-9615-5345-6

Printed in the United States of America.

10 9 8 7 6 5 4 3 2 1
95 94 93 92 91 90 89 88

Dedication

Because of my father, Keith Taft, I feel rich. His generosity and practical help in my endeavors have been instrumental in enabling me to develop my writing abilities. His courage, wisdom, and deep faith in God continues still to inspire and challenge me. I love you, Dad.

Because of my mother, Dorothy Taft, I feel loved. She truly has a "mother's heart," whose warmth and hospitality have always made our home a favorite place for friends to gather. No one is more thoughtful or self-sacrificing. I love it when she laughs. I love you, Mom.

Because of my sister-in-law, Ruth, I feel blessed. Her friendship, loyalty and unflinching commitment to God have been a source of great comfort to me. Through her pain, she has developed a depth of understanding and wisdom well beyond her years. I love you, Ruth.

Because of my brother, Marty, I feel encouraged. His enthusiastic, fun-loving nature has made him a joy to grow up with and a continued blessing. His tender heart, analytical ability and sense of fairness have made him a brother I will always look up to. I love you, Marty.

Because of my sister, Jody, I feel grateful. She is intelligent, gifted and gives me sound, practical advice. Through the years, she has faithfully supported my endeavors, and stood beside me when the going got tough. I love you, Jody.

CONTENTS

PART I
TROUBLED WATERS

PART II
A TIME FOR TEARS

PART III
THE FINAL FAREWELL

PART IV
LEARNING TO WALK AGAIN

Special thanks and deepest gratitude to Janice Rogers for her invaluable training and expertise in teaching me the tools to become a better writer, and for her editing help on this book.

I also wish to thank Tom Bragg, for his tremendous support, guidance and belief in me, which has given me the opportunity and freedom to learn so much during my work with Frontline Communications.

PART I

TROUBLED WATERS

*". . . you do not know about tomorrow.
What is your life? For you are a mist that
appears for a little time and then
vanishes" (James 4:14).*

Chapter 1

Broken Dreams

March 20, 1984. A fresh ocean breeze blew in from the kitchen window in front of me. I took a deep breath as it swept through my curls, a welcome relief from the scorching heat that never seemed to let up on the Big Island of Hawaii. But in just three months I'd be leaving behind this town of Kona where I'd been teaching school with Youth With A Mission, an interdenominational group of Christian missionaries.

My mind raced forward to northern California and a cooler summer with my parents. If only we could have more time before my father and two brothers, Marty and Dana, left on their grueling expedition. They would be joining members of their Bible study group on motorcycles to travel all the way from California to Alaska. Both Marty and Dana would be leaving their wives and Marty's two children behind for the month-long adventure. I knew they were excited about the trip but I only hoped they'd be careful and everything would go smoothly. It was such a long and dangerous trip by motorcycle.

To me, nothing seemed more vulnerable than a person on a motorcycle, speeding down a highway with cars and trucks hurtling by. But then, I smiled to myself, surely God would protect a Bible-believing group of Christians on a trip together. Besides, if anything happened, at least they would have Dana around—a certified doctor, after just 10 more months of medical school!

The ringing phone on the counter behind jarred me. Wiping my hands on a towel, I turned to answer it. A long-distance crackle sounded over the wires. "Hello?"

"Renee, it's Jody," a voice answered softly. What an unexpected surprise from my only sister! Jody, just a year younger than me, lived in Dallas, Texas with her husband, Scott. But why was she calling? She'd never phoned me before in Hawaii.

"I've got some sad news," Jody explained, her voice lowering even more. A surge of fear rose in my throat. "Nothing's happened to our family, has it?"

"No."

I heaved a sigh of relief, but only for a moment.

"It's Rhonda." Rhonda. I remembered my visit with her, just a few months ago. We had stayed in touch after college, where she was my roommate and best friend. Now she lived with her husband in Illinois, and in only one month she'd be a mother. It had been so much fun to see her in her maternity clothes. I took a deep breath.

"What about Rhonda?"

"She had a car accident," Jody said slowly. "Rhonda's been killed."

"Oh, no! No!" I fought the truth of what she was saying.

"Her baby! What about her baby?" I gasped.

"Her baby boy only lived an hour," Jody said in a whisper.

Then both of us were silent as the long-distance crackle echoed eerily over the telephone. I tried to take in the cruel news. It couldn't be true! Rhonda was planning to go into seminary to become an ordained minister. She had a husband and a baby on the way. Why her, God? Why?

Jody finally broke the silence and explained that Rhonda had been broadsided in an intersection. She died immediately and therefore the baby's oxygen was cut off.

Jody told me that Rhonda's body would be flown back to her home town for the funeral.

"Do you think you'll go to the funeral, Renee?"

"No," I said quickly. "I couldn't face it. Besides, I don't think I'd be much help to her family."

I mumbled goodbye to my sister and mechanically dialed my parent's home in California. Soon the soft, pleasant voice of my mother, Dorothy, came over the receiver.

"Oh, Mom, it's Renee! Have you heard?"

"Jody has already told me."

For the first time, tears began to make their way down my cheeks. "It's still so hard to believe!" I blurted.

As my mother and I talked about Rhonda's death, a deep fear began to invade me. *How easily death can invade your life.* It could have been my parents or even Marty, Dana or Jody. Tragedy had never struck so close before, and now I felt helpless and afraid.

"Mom, could you imagine one of your own children ever dying?" But before she could respond I had the most horrible thought. "Mom, just think how you'd feel if Dana were ever flown home in a coffin!"

My mother's groan made me instantly regret the words. After all, she had spent her life staying home and sacrificing for her children. In five quick years, by the time she was 24, there were four of us to take care of. I was sure her "mother's heart" made the thought of losing a child inconceivable. Besides, why did I say "Dana"? Maybe it was because he was the baby of the family and I instinctively felt more protective of him.

Of course, there was certainly no reason for me to protect Dana. In undergraduate school, they used to call him "John the Baptist" with his long, gangly walk, wiry brown hair and beard, and the old leather-covered Bible he kept tucked under his arm. Through the years, Dana had always put God before everything else. Soon, he'd be graduating from medical school and dedicating his life to serving people overseas. No. Steady, level-headed Dana was definitely not someone I needed to worry about.

My mother and I talked on, and before hanging up the receiver, she encouraged me to fly to Rhonda's funeral. But I hedged. For one thing, I had my teaching responsibilities. But there was an even deeper reason for my reluctance and I knew it. I felt so ill-equipped. What would I say to Rhonda's husband, Bill, and the rest of her family? What words of comfort could I possibly bring? And what could I do to help ease their sorrow anyway? Besides, I didn't want to see Rhonda's body. Even if her coffin were closed, it would still hurt just to be there. And that was a reality I did not want to confront.

I gazed blankly out the open window, but now the ocean breeze brought no comfort, no relief. Instead, a blanket of despair settled over me. I stumbled upstairs and fell across my bed. It just didn't seem possible. Rhonda was the one I went to for comfort and advice. Rhonda was the one who said all she wanted was a godly husband and a ministry to serve God. Why then, had this happened? Had God just let her accidentally slip through His fingers? Was He powerless to prevent such a terrible mistake? Did He really care about us?

I rolled over on my back as tears of reality made their way down my cheeks. Like a frightened little girl, I curled up into a ball and tried not to think about it. I had always felt so safe as a Christian, but now everything seemed so dark and empty. I wanted to retreat into some dream world. Finally, I fell asleep.

Turning over in bed the next morning, I couldn't place what was wrong. Then it hit me. Rhonda was dead. Later that day I bought a sympathy card for her husband—a picture of Jesus as the Good Shepherd tenderly looking down and holding one of His sheep.

But what could I write on it? Painstakingly I scribbled a few lines of my love and sorrow over losing Rhonda and shoved it into a mailbox.

During the next few months, I did everything I could to put it out of my mind, trying to deny my sorrow over

Rhonda's death. I buried deep all the questions that had crept into my mind as I escaped into my work.

I threw myself even more into my teaching responsibilities, comfortably hiding behind work and activity to prevent any such thoughts from surfacing.

One spring day as lunch time arrived, I was unexpectedly called into my principal's office. Stepping inside, I smiled as I sat down in front of her desk. But escaping my gaze, she quickly looked down. *Something was wrong!*

"Renee, I have some sad news. It's Wilma." I looked at her quizzically. A 24-year-old Canadian, Wilma had been a fellow teacher with me. Now she and her husband were in Africa with our mission, and she'd just given birth to their first child.

Tears came to the principal's eyes. "Wilma had an asthma attack in Africa. She died." Stunned, I stared at her. How could it be? Not again! Another one—young and dedicated to God's service was swept from this earth.

Quickly excusing myself, I escaped to the lunchroom. But I couldn't shake my heaviness. I listlessly went about my duties. First Rhonda, and now Wilma—I couldn't put it out of my mind. Life seemed so wooden now.

As the weeks went by and the Hawaiian nights grew hotter, I longed for school to end so I could head home for California. In May a letter from Rhonda's husband, Bill arrived. It was hard to think of him as a widower. Grabbing a chair at the kitchen table and shoving aside the lunch dishes, I began to read:

> *Renee, do you play chess? If you've ever played chess you know the importance of the Queen. If you lose the Queen, you frequently lose the game or at least feel like you will lose the game. Sometimes you are so busy moving the pawns, bishops, and knights, you forget about the possibility of losing the Queen. You assume the Queen will be there beside you with every move. Suddenly, out of*

*nowhere, you lose your Queen and the game
seems lost. Rhonda was my Queen—a most
wonderful Queen. For the last several weeks
the game seemed lost. My Queen gone, the
game did not appear to be worth playing.*

I stopped reading. Was life just a game, a game of chance?

Folding the letter neatly and placing it back in the envelope, I looked out through the limp kitchen curtains at the gray ocean. Heavy clouds hung above the water. The stifling midday heat seemed more intense than usual. Once again, I felt enveloped by a thick blanket. I felt like running away but there was no escape. I had always believed in a sovereign, intimate God who knew the number of the hairs on my head and who saw every sparrow fall. Before, it had been easy for me to spout these beliefs, but now I wasn't so sure. Nervously, I stood and picked up my dirty dishes and walked to the kitchen sink, turning on the faucet. As the onslaught of water whirled down the drain, all I could do was stare numbly.

Chapter 2

Preparation

Early one morning, a few weeks later, I reached for the phone. My brother, Dana, attended medical school in Tulsa, Oklahoma, and today was June 2nd, his 26th birthday. But besides wanting to wish him a happy birthday, I also hoped he could provide some answers to the fears still plaguing me. He had seemed so full of faith in recent months, really taking his Christianity seriously. At our last Christmas gathering, he had even confided how he hadn't put God first in undergraduate school, and was getting a second chance now in medical school. Every day now, he tried to spend two hours in prayer and Bible study.

As his phone began to ring, I couldn't help thinking maybe Dana was being a little extreme. After all, he had his whole life ahead of him. Certainly God could understand why Dana couldn't devote great amounts of time to Him when he needed to be studying. Besides, Dana would later be serving God overseas as a medical missionary.

We all knew Dana had been deeply challenged by reading the journals of a missionary named Jim Elliot, published after his death. Back in the 1950's, Jim, along with four other men, had been martyred at a young age by the Auca Indians in Equador. I smiled as I remembered how challenged Dana had been by one of the journal entries:

> My grades came through this week and
> were, as expected, lower than last
> semester. However, I make no apologies
> and admit I've let them drag a bit for study
> of the Bible, in which I seek the degree
> A.U.G. – "Approved unto God."[1]

The words fit Dana to a "t", but I hoped he didn't let his grades drag too much.

A voice on the other end of the phone brought me back to the present. Ruth, Dana's wife, said she'd bring him to the phone. A thoughtful, petite brunette and a committed Christian herself, Ruth was working to help put Dana through medical school. I knew she had also been affected by the writings of Jim Elliot's wife, Elisabeth, and had even told me how she wept as she read about Jim's martyrdom. Elisabeth's devotion to God had deeply challenged her. "Imagine," she had said, "to have the strength and maturity that Elisabeth Elliot had at such a young age—and as a widow!"

Ruth herself had lost her sister and two nephews in a car accident a few years before, and then last year, her mother suffered a devastating divorce. Yes, Ruth had certainly known her share of sorrows, yet she had once confided no matter what the cost, she wanted the same love and uncompromising allegiance to the Lord that Elisabeth had. She had even written it in her journal.

Dana's groggy voice came over the receiver—he'd been taking a nap. After birthday congratulations and talk over some of his course work, I hesitantly brought up Rhonda's death.

"I guess God just allowed the accident," I mumbled, aware of the old despair settling over me again.

Dana's voice rose a bit. "Renee, God doesn't make mistakes."

"You don't think so?" I asked with some surprise.

"Absolutely not!" he resounded. *How could Dana be so definite about God's sovereignty in our lives?*

Feeling a bit uncomfortable, I changed the subject,

telling him how much I looked forward to his medical school graduation—I couldn't believe it was only months away! But then Dana became quiet for a moment. "To tell you the truth, Renee, I'm really not looking forward to it." I was amazed to hear the disappointment in his voice.

"Why not?" I asked, letting out a little laugh of unbelief.

"Well, Renee . . . it's because of the glory and recognition I'll receive."

Now Dana was really taking things too far. After nine years of schooling, he deserved some recognition. I, for one, was so proud. Imagine, my little brother a doctor!

A few minutes later, I hung up and sat staring at the phone. I wished I could have Dana's faith. I thought back to Rhonda's husband talking about chess and losing his Queen, and right then, I again felt life was nothing but a game—a game of chance where the odds remained uncertain.

I knew I had to get up and get busy. I would leave Hawaii for California in just a few weeks and there was much to do. But still I sat there, still looking at that phone, still hearing Dana's words. Instead of giving me answers, his attitude had further deepened my doubts.

I stood and looked out the window and watched the waves of the ocean rise up regally in my view, only to come crashing down again and again. I shuddered and prayed that no more unexpected torrents would ever come crashing down my way again.

3

Chapter 3

On Their Way

It was nine o'clock on the night of July 4th, after an unusually quiet day. Ordinarily our family would have spent the day getting ready for a picnic or something, but this year was different. The men— Dad, Dana and my older brother, Marty—were on that motorcycle tour up in Canada with their men's Bible study group, on their way to Alaska. Marty's family had spent the day with his wife's relatives and Mom and I had gone shopping here in Sunnyvale. Now I sat flipping the channels of the television set in front of me with the remote control, only to find nothing on. I'd only been home from Hawaii a week and already time was hanging heavy on my hands.

The phone rang in the kitchen and I watched Mom reach for it. At 50, she was still attractive with her blonde hair, laughing blue eyes and curvaceous Dutch build.

"Hi, honey," she chirped, and I knew it was Dad. Mom glanced over at me and smiled reassuringly. Everything must be going well on their journey. Still I wished I felt really content. The Fourth had always been a family affair. I missed the rest of the family and it was only five days into their month-long trip.

Turning my head around and resting it on the recliner, I thought how disappointed I'd been at not spending enough time with Dana before he left. Busy getting ready for their camping trip, Dana had reassured me there'd be lots of time together when they got back at the end of the summer before his clerkships began in a nearby hospital. Of course, I knew he was right. If his understanding wife, Ruth, could manage to stay home in Tulsa and work for the summer without seeing him for two more months, surely I could be patient for a few more weeks. And Ruth could rest easy about one thing. Since Dana knew he misplaced things easily, he had entrusted Mom with his treasured wedding ring, just in case he lost it. Mom had safely put the large gold ring, engraved with a dove and cross, in a porcelain cup and tucked it away in her china cabinet.

At least my dad and brothers wouldn't be driving motorcycles. They had elected to take the station wagon to carry supplies for the group, making the journey far safer and more comfortable, besides providing them some real family time together.

All three had always been close. Marty, five years older than Dana, stood 6'7, and with his thick, curly mop of blond hair, he was someone a younger brother could "look up to." Marty was a born teacher, and had taught Dana everything from electronics to mechanics from the time he was small. They loved to experiment and tinker with projects together. And my dad, Keith, squarely built and full of life, also loved to try new things. Married to my mother at just 18, Dad was still young at heart as well as in body.

Mom got off the phone and heaved a sigh of relief. "They're having a great time," she said as she put the kettle on. I hastily pulled up a chair at the kitchen table as she leaned against the stove. "They are in a little town called Hazelton, just 100 miles from the Alaskan border."

The kettle began to whistle and now Mom poured herself a cup of coffee. "Oh, and they just bought a rubber raft for themselves," she added.

I shuddered a little as I thought back to the time when I was just a teenager, heading downstream in a raft with my brother, Marty. The raft quickly filled with water in the strong current, and as I paddled to the side, I grabbed for a tree branch to stop us. Suddenly we were in the rushing water, and the raft was beyond my reach. Marty managed to cling to it but I began drifting farther and farther away. Frantically, I fought to stay afloat as the water threatened to engulf me, until I shouted at the top of my lungs to God.

"Help me! Save me, God!" I cried. Just then, Marty extended his long arm to where he heard my shouting. Spotting his hand, I grabbed it and he pulled me to the raft. Trembling in fear, we maneuvered our way back to a calm and shallow place in the river and stumbled onto shore.

From that day on, Marty had always been leery of rafts, but I knew how much Dana loved the water. Even when he was a child, he would pretend he was a fish and see how long he could hold his breath under water. He would practice and practice until he could swim three times the length of our small pool without coming up for air. Often, he built rafts supported on pontoons and went out on a nearby lake with his friends. Yes, rafting was something that would really make this trip special for him.

Soon it was time for bed, marking the end of a dull Fourth of July. My mom and I mechanically made our way down the hall to our rooms for the night. I yawned as I prepared for bed and fell on top of the covers, too hot for any blanket. But for some reason, sleep escaped me. I began to toss and turn. My eyes wide awake, I gazed out through my bedroom window at the blaze of firecrackers lighting up the sky. I heard the sound of my mother's bedroom door creak open and her feet padding down the hall. Soon I could hear her pacing back and forth on the patio outside my room.

She must be restless too, I thought. I strained to see the hands on my wristwatch and sighed. Over 30 minutes had passed since I'd gone to bed. The fireworks were beginning to bother me. Everywhere it seemed, people were celebrating the Fourth. How I wished that my father and brothers were here, so we could enjoy it too! I rolled over on my back as I pictured being with all of them again in just a few weeks. What a reunion that would be! But until then, I couldn't help thinking about the fun they must be having even now, riding in a rubber raft amidst the beautiful Canadian wilds.

Chapter 4

Stepping On Shore
And Finding It Heaven

The next evening Mom and I sat entranced, our eyes wide with growing suspense at the TV movie. A young, athletic man had been dog paddling in the middle of the ocean for five hours without a life jacket. As we watched his arm motion slow in the cold, dark water, we knew he couldn't last much longer. My mother shifted in her chair, her mouth set in a grim line. "This is making me nervous. I wish someone would do something!"

Abruptly I heard the sliding glass door open, and I jumped with a start. The movie forgotten, I whirled around. *It was Dad!* I let out my breath, then thought, *What's he doing home so soon? He was supposed to be gone for a month!* Shuffling in behind him was Marty, his wife Rosie, and their two children. *But why are they all here at nine o'clock at night? And where is Dana? Something is wrong!*

With a cautious look on his face, Dad approached my mother and gently placed his hand on her shoulder. She tensed. "We've had an accident," Dad whispered. "Dana's gone to be with the Lord."

No, it couldn't be! My mind couldn't take the words

in. I watched transfixed as my mother shot out of her seat and cried out, "No! Not my precious boy! Tell me it's not true! No! No! What happened?"

"He drowned."

My mouth dropped opened as I gasped in disbelief. I stared at my mother as her face contorted in anguish. She turned and began to pace through the living room, wringing her hands. "No! No! No! No!" The agony in her voice chilled me.

I still couldn't believe it. It was so much like watching the characters in the movie we had been watching. My dad stood helplessly. Marty and his wife, Rosie, watched Mom's torment, with tears running down their cheeks. I watched as Marty's eyes glanced from face to face, then to a picture of a remote control airplane he and Dana had built together. Was he thinking of the hours he and his buddy had spent, sprawled out here with some project? Now his buddy was gone. No longer would they be able to share the hobbies and interests they had so enjoyed together.

Marty gently countered my mother's stream of denials with an explanation. "Yesterday, Dad and Dana decided to ride the raft toward our campground," he began shakily. "I drove down river and stood on a bridge waiting with the video camera as they approached. They planned to get off there."

"Did you have life jackets on?" Mom snapped as she looked at Dad. He shook his head.

"No," Dad replied softly. "But the river was calm. And there was a rope surrounding the raft just in case we did capsize." Dad's eyes glanced downward. "Dana just didn't grab it in time."

Dad went on to describe the exhilarating 20-minute journey he and Dana had as they approached the bridge. "It was so peaceful. The sun was just going down behind the mountains; the water was so smooth. Dana and I just stared around us, taking in God's creation." Dad's voice dropped and his eyes got a faraway look. "It was so beautiful." He let out a big sigh. "It was then we decided to continue on past the bridge until we reached the campground...."

After a heavy silence, Marty picked up the story. "I saw the raft like a tiny speck heading toward me, and began videotaping. It got bigger and bigger until I saw Dad and Dana. Then, the water got suddenly swift in one little section and I saw . . . the raft just flipped."

Marty said he watched in horror as Dad and Dana were swept instantly apart in the swirling water. Seeing that Dana was only 20 feet from shore and knowing he was a strong swimmer, for a moment he focused on Dad hanging onto the raft. When Dad yelled he was fine and to get Dana, Marty looked back but Dana had vanished.

"I ran down a steep bank, crying out loud for God to save Dana but I . . . I couldn't find him anywhere," Marty stammered, choking back the tears.

"If only I could have helped," Dad said brokenly. He went on to explain how he hung on atop the capsized raft as it floated down the river in the rapidly dimming light. Steering with his hands, Dad guided the raft by the sounds of the stream, avoiding the sound of loud rushing water when he came to a fork. An hour later and 10 miles down river, Dad saw lights from the little town of Hazelton and paddled toward shore. After getting out, he raced back along the river in the dark where the accident occurred.

"When I saw the station wagon driving along, I ran up to find only Marty get out." A long pause followed as we faced the terrible truth. "We waited until light," Dad said heavily. "Helicopters, rescue men and the Bible study group were all looking for him." He looked at the floor. "We finally had to give up."

Marty said the Royal Canadian Mounted Police were investigating the accident so he gave them the video tape. "Maybe it'll help them find him," he said with hope in his voice. Dad explained they had left the station wagon in Hazelton to fly home to California as soon as possible, and encouraged the others in the Bible study group to continue on their journey.

Although my father's eyes were moist, his voice was firm and steady. "There was such peace on Dana's face the last glimpse I caught of him. Somehow I don't think this was just an accident."

Numbly, I reached my arm around my dad and whispered that I was grateful he was still alive. But my mother could not conceal her grief and had no time for theology. Her face was drawn and her mouth quivered as she flew to the kitchen phone and dialed a friend from church. "Martha!" she wailed, "I've lost my boy! My precious boy is gone!"

Mom hung up the phone a minute later, stammering that Martha was notifying the pastor and coming over with him shortly. As we waited, Mom continued to deny that Dana was dead.

"It can't be true!" she kept saying. Just months earlier, Mom had told me she could never handle the death of any of her children. Now the unthinkable had happened. Now it hit her head-on. *Would God help her survive the blast?*

Pacing the living room again, Mom's voice rose in anger. "Why would God let my son die when he had so much to offer here on earth?" "Why weren't His guardian angels on the alert?" *If onlys* were fired in rapid succession. *If only* they had stopped at the bridge, it would never have happened. *If only* the raft had been over one foot closer to the middle of the river, it wouldn't have capsized. *If only* they had had on life jackets, he might have lived. *If only* Dana had grabbed the rope that surrounded the raft like her husband had, he would have survived. *If only*, she pleaded, she could have her son back.

For me the reality of Dana's death still had not registered with me. My eyes were dry and I was sure I'd be fine. I could not perceive the intensity of pain I was to experience in the coming days, weeks and months. I was unaware I had a horrible wound festering underneath the surface, just about to be torn wide open. I would find the wound so gaping, so deep and so hurtful that the healing process would take far longer than I could have ever anticipated. Without the grace and comfort of God as He taught us the milestones of grief, I don't know if my family and I could've survived it.

My sister, Jody and her husband, Scott, in Dallas, hadn't been told yet. Neither had Ruth, Dana's wife, waiting in Tulsa for him to return from his trip. How could we tell Ruth that her husband of only three years had died? Yes, she knew the ache of losing loved ones and seeing her parents divorce. She worked hard each day at her lab job to help Dana through medical school, waiting to start a family until he graduated. And now this!

Marty went to the kitchen phone to break the news to Jody and Scott. I sank onto the sofa and listened as he asked if they would drive the five hours from Dallas to Tulsa to tell Ruth in person. My last phone conversation with Ruth came to mind, when she'd talked about Elisabeth Elliot's book on her husband's martyrdom by the Aucas. Elisabeth's example had so challenged her, and now, at just 26, not much younger than Elisabeth Elliot had been, Ruth was facing the same loss of a husband. Was that why she had just read that book? *Had God somehow been preparing Ruth all along?*

Marty hung up and reported that my sister and her husband would leave tonight to drive to Ruth's. They wanted to be there before Ruth left for work in the morning, so she didn't hear the news from the Canadian police.

Soon my parents' friends and pastor rang the bell. Still trembling, my mother opened the door and the small living room filled with people. Martha threw her arms around Mom, who began to sob in convulsions. Dad's eyes filled with tears as he walked toward our guests and took the pastor's outstretched hand. Everyone settled down in muted conversation, but I was in no mood for company. The room was suddenly too crowded and hot. Even though my ears heard our friends' words of sympathy, all I wanted to do was get away.

Escaping to my bedroom, I buried my head in my pillow. But there was nowhere to run from the horrible truth.

With each new minute that passed, there came certain and deeper realization that Dana had really died. I wanted to fight the facts because reality was simply too painful to accept. Besides, there was still a shred of hope—they hadn't found his body, and so maybe Dana was wandering somewhere along the shore. Maybe he even had amnesia. Maybe he was unconscious and couldn't look for help.

Only God and my pillow knew how many tears I cried that night. I sobbed until I sank into exhausted sleep, but only moments later my muscles tensed and I jerked awake as "Dana's dead" screamed over and over in my head. On and on it went—crying, oblivion, waking to cruel thoughts—until the dawn began to break outside my window. I didn't know it, but in coming weeks, I would find waking from sleep the most vulnerable part of my day. Always I would hope it wasn't real, that it had only been a dream. But then there'd come that twisting reminder that the nightmare was reality. How I would pray the clock could be turned back, that there could be some way to change what had happened.

But now, on that horrible night of July 5th, I groaned as I thrashed on my bed, and anxious thoughts raced and repeated in my mind. I looked at the time—2:30 a.m. Jody and Scott would be at Dana's apartment soon to tell his wife, Ruth. *Would she ever be able to survive and accept the loss of her husband?*

Throwing my pillow over my head, as if to shut out the pain, I refused to accept what had happened. Over and over I could hear echo in my mind words spoken that night by a well-meaning friend: "Dana's in heaven. Dana's in heaven." But the thought wasn't comforting. I didn't want Dana in heaven. I wanted him here with us!

Chapter 5
Your Husband Is Now Your Maker

The phone rang before dawn, jarring me out of half-sleep. Struggling to wake up, a rock in the pit of my stomach reminded me. Dana was dead.

I lumbered to my bedroom door and cracked it open. I could hear Mom's strained voice in the hallway on the phone, and I realized it was my sister, Jody.

My mother hung up the phone and came to me, her face drawn and tear-stained. Quivering, she whispered that Dana's wife, Ruth, had been told and she, Jody, and Scott would take the next flight to California. I wrapped my arms around her and she began to cry out again her disbelief over her son's death.

My parent's bedroom door creaked and Dad's face appeared. He smiled tenderly at me, but his sad eyes showed he was hurting too. We went to the kitchen and slumped at the table while Mom started up the kettle. An empty day lay ahead for us. There was nothing to do but wait for Scott, Jody and Ruth to arrive. It wasn't until later that day that Jody would show me her journal describing what had taken place that painful morning when Ruth was first told of her husband's death:

When Scott and I knocked on the door of the

apartment that Dana and Ruth had shared, Ruth's voice was full of concern.

"Who is it?" she called, sounding bewildered and sleepy.

"It's Jody," was all I managed to say, wondering if she would be able to place the name when she wasn't expecting to see me.

The door opened immediately and Ruth, dressed in a pale blue robe, blinking the sleep out of her eyes, asked, "Is everything all right?"

"No," I replied, placing my arm around her, "it isn't. Dana's dead."

I couldn't think of any other way of saying it. Later that day I found out my father had broken the news to my mother with the words, "Dana's gone to be with the Lord." I wished I had thought of those words as they seemed so much more appropriate.

Despite my ineptness, Ruth asked us to sit down, asked for the details and made herself a cup of coffee. As I watched her, I marveled at the strength she had in the Lord. Ruth said simply she hadn't wanted Dana to go rafting and she wished he hadn't gone. I never again heard her utter a word of "if only."

We flew out of Tulsa a few hours later with Ruth shedding only a few tears. The deep grief I knew she must be feeling was being held in check firmly by her desire to be strong in the Lord.

We didn't realize it then, but four of us began journals during those days immediately following Dana's death. We would later find these written accounts to be invaluable.

While on the plane heading for California, Ruth wrote in her journal:

> *There was a knock at the door. It was Jody, Dana's sister. Dana has drowned in a rafting accident. Oh, Lord, Thou knowest and searchest all! Thou who scrutinizes my path and art intimately acquainted with all my ways. You be glorified, Jesus. Keep me in Thy hand. Let me glorify You in my speech and conduct. I lift my grieving up to You, that it would be according to Your will. I desire to be appropriate in Thy sight. Oh, spirit of God, guide me as I go. Let this be a turning point in all our lives. I love You, Jesus. I commend my life to You. Do as You will, Lamb of God. Yet I will trust in Thee.*

Like Ruth, we would all learn God's guidance through the valley of the shadow of death. Though I didn't see it at the time, God was gently guiding us on the pathway through grieving, step by step.

in the Lord.

We didn't realize it then, but [illegible] during the weeks immediately following Dan's death, we would have had [illegible] moments [illegible] the [illegible] for Christmas [illegible] wrote in her journal:

> Lord, we were [illegible] at the door [illegible] Dan's [illegible] Thank You [illegible] who [illegible] my back and [illegible] You are [illegible] Keep me in Your hand [illegible] would be according to Your will [illegible] in Thy sight. [illegible] be a turning point in all our lives. [illegible] my life to You [illegible] Lamb of God. Yet I will [illegible]

In truth, we would all learn God's guidance through the valley of the shadow of death. Though I didn't [illegible] at the time, God was gently guiding us [illegible] through [illegible] step by step.

Chapter 6

The First Milestone

My parents and I waited anxiously at the airport late the morning of July 6th. Only eight days earlier, Dana had flown in from Tulsa and just being at the airport again heightened the cruel truth. Soon I spotted Jody with her husband, Scott, heading toward me from the plane. Jody's square jaw was set firmly as she gazed at me through misty, wide-set blue eyes. Throwing my arms around her, I buried my head in her blonde locks. My parents headed toward Ruth, a few feet behind, and soon our family clumped in the aisle of the airport, crying un-ashamedly. For the first time I heard Dad cry great, racking sobs of grief.

Then I remembered Dana's words to me—spoken months earlier when my friend, Rhonda had been killed. "Renee," he had said, "God doesn't make mistakes." As I told the others, we clung to those words, later to be repeated over and over again by all of us.

As Jody, Scott and Ruth waited for their baggage, my brother, Marty arrived, along with his wife and two children. Unconsciously I counted as I usually did at family gatherings. But it was 10 instead of 11. Only one person was missing: Dana. Never again would the family seem complete. How I longed to see his smiling, rock-steady countenance.

Of the 10 of us, one was a marvel—Dana's widow, Ruth. Serene and composed, she was a private person and didn't readily show her emotions, but an amazing peace seemed to penetrate from her soft green eyes. This certainly wasn't the broken widow I anticipated. Perhaps the full impact still hadn't hit her yet. But on the other hand, had God been mysteriously preparing her for this day?

As we arrived back from the airport, cars were lined up in front of our cream-colored tract home. Relatives and friends had already begun to filter in, rallying around us with love and support. Ruth's mother came and Dad's parents flew in from Montana. As Grandma and Grandpa Taft expressed how deeply they felt our pain, their own story came to my mind. Thirty years before, their only daughter died in a freak accident at only nine years old. Without warning, a basketball board in the school gymnasium broke loose from the wall, hitting her in the heart and knocking her unconscious. She died soon after. Now, for the first time, I could relate to the heartbreak of that story I'd known since childhood.

That day we had as much food as people in our home, but my stomach turned just seeing the ham, roast beef and bountiful desserts. No one ever told me grief could produce such a sick, nauseating feeling. No one ever told me how meaningless eating and even living felt when you've just lost someone you loved so deeply. And no one ever told me I would hurt so much.

I just wanted to escape. Wasn't there someone I could talk to who had suffered a similar loss? Then an idea struck! Grabbing the hallway phone and carrying it to my bedroom, I dialed the mother of my friend, Rhonda, who died in the car accident. Rhonda's mom would understand! Of course she could identify with us! For the first time since Rhonda's death, I wasn't afraid to call and say the wrong thing. Now I, too, suffered from the agonizing, cutting wound of grief, and somehow I felt sharing our grief could help. I would later realize it was the first milestone God revealed in how to get through the grieving.

Then Rhonda's mom answered the phone. "Mrs. Robson, this is Renee . . . ." Suddenly, a fresh stream of tears began to flow down my face and I blurted out what had happened. I could sense her deep empathy for my loss, and soon we were pouring out our tears and sorrow together. Even over the phone, our hearts became knitted closely.

I put the receiver down 30 minutes later and for the first time, I made my way back into the kitchen with a lighter step. But I stopped in my tracks as I saw the helpless look etched on my mother's face, bent in torment. She continued to vent her "if onlys" to friends and relatives gathered in the kitchen, and even their gentle hands and words of comfort were no use. It was clear her mother's heart had been ripped wide open.

In the dining room nearby, I heard Dad, Ruth and several friends planning the memorial service to be held the following morning. A shudder swept through me. I could never participate in a service that only brought more certainty to Dana's death. Turning away, I darted out of earshot and retreated to my bedroom again, throwing myself on the bed and burying my head in the pillow. Oh God, surely he must be alive somewhere! Please, please bring my brother back. Please let Dana be alive!

Chapter 7

A Time For Remembering

That same jagged rock I'd felt before was lodged in the pit of my stomach as I made my way inside the Baptist Church in Sunnyvale. Even the bright rays of the California sunshine couldn't cheer me. For it was July 9th—five days since Dana's death. And now his memorial service was about to begin, as we all stared reality in the face.

I braced my shoulders and stared straight ahead as I walked down the long stone aisle to the front. Joining the rest of my family, I saw flowers lining the front of the church but no coffin. Dana's body still hadn't been found and I was almost relieved. A coffin in front would make it all so final.

Several hundred people were already gathered as I sat by the young and old of our family. I glanced over at Ruth, dressed in a light beige dress, looking calm. I marveled again at her peaceful countenance.

Our pastor opened the service with a few words of scripture. Brave little Ruth, fingering a folded paper, stepped onto the platform and read boldly from Hosea 2:19-20: "I will betroth you to me forever; I will betroth you in righteousness and justice, In love and compassion. I will betroth you in faithfulness, and you will acknowledge the Lord."

"It's my desire," she continued, "that we realize God's wonderful attributes, and that because of Dana's death, each of us would enter into a deeper knowledge of the Lord and a greater understanding of the Father's heart."

Certainly Ruth's faith hadn't been shaken. In spite of now losing her husband, not to mention her sister and two nephews before, Ruth still held firmly to her belief in a loving, Father God who cares about each one of us in intimate detail.

Ruth's brother, Andy, read Dana's favorite entry from Jim Elliot's journal:

> Only I know that my own life is full. It is time to die, for I have had all a young man can have—at least, all *this* young man can have.

As he read, I remembered how many times Dana had talked about Jim Elliot, another young Christian cut off in his prime. *Why had there been such a heart link between Dana and this missionary, dead now for over 30 years?* But now another protest swelled inside me—Dana had his whole life ahead of him as a doctor and was almost ready to put his training to use. But just then my inner objections were answered as Andy continued:

> If there were no further issue from my training, it would be well—the training has been good and to the glory of God. I am ready to meet Jesus. Failure means nothing now, only that it taught me life. Success is meaningless, only that it gave me further experience for using the great gift of God—*life*. And Life, I love thee, not because thou art long, or because thou hast done great things for me, but simply because I have thee from God. [2]

I swallowed hard. How unbelievable! But hadn't Ruth

told me, just three days ago when she arrived, that Dana had so embraced this passage? He had sat one evening in his favorite armchair, reading it aloud to her with tears in his eyes. By the strange look on his face, she sensed he was reading about himself.

That night, Ruth had even gone to see a friend, distraught and needing to talk about Dana's strange attitude. After all, Dana loved life and lived it to the fullest—and more importantly, they had a wonderful life together! She felt uncomfortable for him to be so ready to die.

My mind went to the words of a fellow medical student of Dana's who had flown in for the service. In the last couple of months, Dana had told him the greatest day would be when he saw Jesus face to face. Again I had to wonder. Had God somehow been mysteriously preparing Dana for their early meeting?

My eyes swept down the pew. My tender-hearted brother, Marty, sat beside his wife and two children with quiet teardrops trickling down his face. His only beloved brother was gone.

And Mom, a gentle person, always so compassionate and thoughtful of others, could not conceal her grief today. My sister, Jody, placed her arm around Mom to offer comfort and support. I watched as my mother's eyes closed as if trying to let God touch her through the stream of testimonies, exhortations and scripture readings.

Then I could feel the quiet presence of my dad on the row behind me, next to the aisle. With Dad, there seemed to be no *if's* when it came to his trust in God—even now. He had shared earlier that he felt God's angels were working overtime during the night of the accident. He was sure one of them skillfully protected and guided him to safety while another one ushered Dana into the presence of Jesus. He told me God had mapped and charted their course, and that from one Canadian river out of the stream of all humanity, God had chosen to take Dana for His purposes.

But still I knew my father was hurting, despite his unshakable faith. As the memorial service came to a close, a taped song began to play. Dad's and Dana's melodious voices filled the church as they sang one of their favorites, "Seek Only Thy Perfect Way:"

> I long to be able to enter your city,
> And be near the living God,
> Where even the sparrow can go and is wel-
> come,
> To nest among altars of love.

A stifled sob came from behind me and I turned and watched my father cup his head in his hands amidst the harmonious strains. I rose and tiptoed over to Dad. Kneeling in the aisle, I placed my arm around him, resting my head on his shoulder:

> I sing in the morning a song of thanksgiving,
> For blessings He promised would be,
> 'Til someday ascending He calls to His city,
> All those who in Him have believed.

Dana was home now—called to His eternal heavenly city where he could offer up songs of thanksgiving to a God he knew and loved. And now, more than anything, Dana's desire to see Him had finally, inexplicably, been fulfilled.

As the service ended, I felt an unexpected lift envelop me. We'd passed another milestone of grief. I gazed at my family and saw the same freshness in their eyes, as though an invisible peace had descended upon all of us. After many hugs, extended sympathies and support, my family and I stepped lightly out of the church. The memorial service I had dreaded had been an important healing agent. Our shared faith in the face of life's darkest storm had brought a glimmer of light.

For the first time I began to feel at ease with so many people around. But as I stepped out into the sunshine my smile froze as I recognized a woman straight ahead. She was the wife of one of the Bible study members, who were still continuing their trip in Alaska. The woman had come to our home daily with some little gift of food. But somehow her presence today as well as that of the other wives from the group, only accentuated their husbands' absence.

Why weren't they here? I complained silently. How could they all be on vacation, enjoying themselves, while my precious brother's body floated down some Canadian river? Didn't they realize the biting, agonizing grief we carried? Didn't they want to stand by us in our greatest time of need? I darted past her and stumbled to our car.

Slumping in my seat, I waited for the family as I struggled to put aside the growing waves of bitterness. But then, I thought, why shouldn't I be bitter? Such an incredible ache, like a band around my chest tightened its grip like nothing I'd ever known before.

Even my mother had earlier expressed anger over the Bible study group, flailing about for a target for the frustration and pain. She couldn't understand why they didn't comprehend her pain and suffering and chose to continue their trip. She was angry they chose not to share in our sorrow by standing with us, and vented her feelings in no uncertain words. "If only we'd never known about that Bible study, this wouldn't have happened!" she let out. *If onlys* had now become a regular part of her vocabulary.

But later I would learn God designed stages of grief that we all pass through naturally. We were angry because we were grieving, even though our anger was irrationally focused on this group. We weren't being fair, of course. If we had been in that Bible study group, would we have wanted to turn back from a trip we had looked forward to and planned for so many months? Unless you've lost someone and experienced the devastation and suffering, it's easy to respond to someone else's loss inappropriately.

I certainly had not responded supportively when my friend, Rhonda died. Instead of going to her funeral, I made excuses and yet the slightest insensitivity from others now made me react out of deep hurt and self-pity. I guess I was so vulnerable, so bruised and broken inside, that my vision was blurred. I could only see the speck in someone else's eye but was unaware of the log in my own.

After the service, we arrived back at home to find it filled with close family members. Now Mom's face looked happier and I watched as she handed her sister a cup from the china cabinet. As Mom turned to get the kettle, her sister said curiously, "Why, Dorothy, there's a ring in this cup."

Mom's hand flew over her mouth as her new composure crumbled into sobs. "It's Dana's ring!" she cried.

Dana's ring. He had left it for Mom to take care of, in case he lost it—and now it rattled in the hard china, a reminder of our terrible loss.

Then Mom rallied. "It'll make Ruth happy," she sniffled, trying to produce a smile. Dear Mom. Even in her grief she was thinking of others.

But now Ruth was going through struggles on this unknown course. As she and I huddled in the dining room, she confided how she couldn't understand why she felt a curious mixture of strength mixed with a cold void of no feeling. I didn't know what to say. And because we were all going through this unfamiliar terrain of grief, I didn't know how to prevent what happened next.

Looking somewhat refreshed after our talk, Ruth said she wanted to attend to some business matters pertaining to Dana's school loans. Grabbing the phone, she dialed the financial aid department at Dana's university. After a few minutes, Ruth's green eyes clouded and she hung up, her face ashen.

"They need his . . . death certificate before they'll take care of the debt," she mumbled, jarred by the reality of the words.

Of course we didn't have a death certificate yet. Since Dana's body had not been recovered, the Canadian police had said it could take several months to obtain one.

Ruth sank back into the chair. "The reality of his death just hit me and it's hard," she said, choking back the tears. Silently she walked out of the kitchen and headed down the hall.

As I sat numbly at the table, it slowly dawned on me what Ruth had done. She had tried to counter that odd numbness by forcing herself to confront Dana's death. But she wasn't ready—and it was a real error.

All of us needed to allow ourselves an important factor in the healing process—time. Denial, I was finding, was actually a step in the grief process. It protected us from the unbearable pain of too suddenly taking on the full impact of losing Dana. Our denial had varied from our immediate reaction of "Oh, no!" to the often unconscious unwillingness to make decisions that would bring finality to our loss. But facing everything too quickly, it appeared, could bring about the greatest, most raw sorrow we had ever known.

The next morning, Ruth popped into the kitchen where I was eating breakfast, amazingly chipper after our ordeal the previous day.

"What's happened to you, Ruth?" I asked, perplexed.

"After everyone was asleep last night, I got real honest with God and told him how much I hurt. Somehow I knew that I didn't have to be tough anymore and it felt much better." She stopped and smiled.

"Then, I started praising Him and felt so uplifted!"

I looked at her serene face and marveled at how quickly God was teaching us how to face this sorrow. Ruth sat down next to me and began to share that although grief had stripped us of our self-confidence, leaving us needy, weak and helpless, she had learned two important principles that night. As she had gone to God like a little child, He was able to cradle and comfort her through the suffering. Then Ruth made the choice to praise Him, what the Bible speaks of as putting on the "garment of praise for the spirit of heaviness" (Isaiah 61:3 KJV). Ruth had found renewed strength and grace to continue.

I sat quietly, looking at my breakfast plate. Be a child—don't try to be tough—and praise God. Two more major steps.

During the next few days, though, as relatives and friends began to disperse, my family and I found we were left alone to work through our grief and our lives without Dana. We were learning still another lesson in the healing process—how important it is to reach out and draw close as a family, sharing our pain together. We felt safe in knowing that the ache in each of our hearts and the tears that so easily came to our eyes, were received with an understanding nod, a tender hand reaching out or a compassionate hug from one another.

Soon after the crowds began to leave, some of us—my parents, Ruth, Jody, and I—decided to fly to where the accident occurred in Hazelton, British Columbia. Dad planned to retrieve our station wagon, left with a Christian man who worked with the Canadian police who had led the search party for Dana. Therefore, on Friday the 13th, full of dread and hope for healing, we all boarded a plane headed for Hazelton. Friday the 13th never looked so grim.

PART II

A TIME FOR TEARS

"I am weary with my moaning; every night I flood my bed with tears; I drench my couch with weeping. My eye wastes away because of grief..." (Psalm 6:6-7).

Chapter 8

Rocky Mountains

The trees and winding Canadian roads passed in a blur as I peered out of the car window. I was beginning to wish I hadn't come. It had been a hectic day of travel, with missed planes and lost baggage.

Then, after renting a car to make the hour's drive to Hazelton from the airport, Dad had made a wrong turn, taking us 30 miles out of our way. Some might think it was a typical day for Friday the 13th, but it was even harder now that we were driving alongside the Skeena River in which Dana had drowned. A fresh wave of fear swept over me as I saw how shallow it looked. Quickly, I turned my head away, too overwhelmed by the horrible possibility of seeing Dana lying on some beach nearby.

Vulnerability and dread mounted with every twist of the mountain road. No longer did I feel like I had any guarantee against unforeseen events in my life. What suffering or even greater sorrow could lay ahead? I had lost the sense of my own omnipotence—the mistaken belief that I had everything under control and that my future would turn out exactly as I planned. As I glanced around at the quiet, subdued faces of my family—Dad and Mom in the front with Ruth and Jody in the back next to me—I could feel their apprehension too.

I closed my eyes and made myself comfortable, resting my head against the back cushion. At least we had each other. As a family, we were more united than ever and even this trip had truly been a time of "bearing one another's burdens."

Time after time in those tender days, we saw that if one was down, the others lifted him or her up by quoting meaningful scriptures or lending listening ears. Sometimes we read aloud portions of Elisabeth Elliot's books, drawing strength from someone who had walked the same path many years before. Together we could talk frankly about our sorrow and what we had learned, something we often felt too vulnerable to do with our friends for fear of possible rejection or insensitivity. But among our family, we knew we were comfortable with one another's tears and would be received with acceptance.

But even with such encouragement, my sorrow sometimes was so overwhelming I wished I could withdraw into my own world and escape from the gnawing reality of Dana's death.

Our car suddenly jerked to a stop. I opened my eyes and viewed the sleepy town of Hazelton for the first time. Even in the fading sunlight, I could still see snowpeaked mountains and evergreen forests towering behind a rustic motel and a short line of other buildings. I stepped out of the car and took a deep breath of pine and spruce as Dad went into the motel to see if rooms were available. Mom, Jody, Ruth and I stood silently outside gazing in awe at the green and gray beauty unfolding before us. For a moment I could almost believe we were in this picturesque village on a happier errand.

Dad soon appeared with two keys, and we found our rooms. After dropping off our luggage, we drove the few miles out to the station of the Royal Canadian Mounted Police, who investigated the accident and led the search party. A few minutes later we stood huddled inside a small office as we questioned the young brown-uniformed Mountie policeman behind the counter.

"There's a good chance we'll find him," the Mountie said, as if my brother was just a piece of lost evidence—

another statistic in a long line of accidental drownings. "Sometimes it can be a year or two," he went on routinely, "but we feel pretty certain his body will show up. And if it does, we'll need dental charts for positive proof."

His words fell like cold, deadly rain, and my heart dropped to my knees. The young policeman slapped Dana's file shut, adding it to a bulging tray on the counter, and started shuffling his papers.

Why does he need dental charts? I wondered. Then the reason hit me—another cruel reminder of the probable poor condition of my dear brother's body.

I glanced over at Mom, surprised to see her somewhat relaxed. At last Ruth boldly broke the silence. "We know he's in heaven and would rather you not search too hard." The Mountie looked up and eyed her curiously. It was obvious he didn't understand.

"We know Dana is in heaven," Ruth said again. "We don't want his body."

But the Mountie just ignored Ruth's request, and handed Dad the videotape Marty had left with them just after the accident. "This tape isn't very clear," he said cooly. "The coroner will have to investigate further. Without the body, it could take several years to verify his death."

Dad mumbled a disheartened thank you as we limply made our way outside the station. No one spoke in the car —words seemed inadequate to describe the loss etched on each empty face. But did Mom really appear more at peace than before? Had the Mountie somehow given her hope that the body of her son, which had formed inside her womb 26 years earlier, would someday be returned to her?

But quickly I shoved that notion aside. I certainly didn't want anything that would bring home the reality of Dana's death. If it became any more real, I thought I couldn't bear it. I never before comprehended the real, physical pain in grieving. Again, I felt that sharp rock inside, scraping and cutting into my stomach.

Once back at the motel, I went straight to my bed,

even though it was only 8 p.m. Wrapping my arms tightly around me, I plopped down and stared blankly at the ceiling.

I was sharing a room with Jody and Ruth, and while I could hear them talking softly on the bed next to mine, my mind wouldn't leave the police station. Over and over again, the scene replayed before my eyes until I was livid with anger. *How could that Mountie be so cold and unfeeling? How could he treat my brother's death as simply another statistic?* Then he had just dismissed us, shoving Dana's memory in some file drawer! I felt angry at the unfairness of life, and angry at the reality I was facing.

And what about God? Again the horrible question returned. Were accidents and the subsequent suffering they brought simply out of His control? Was He limited in His power by world-wide events that happened accidentally? And if so, did I have any guarantee that any promise He had ever made would come to pass in my life? *Was God,* I wondered, *really God?*

But even in my hot anger, a cool voice of reason persisted. I knew Dana wouldn't have agreed with me. He embraced life as he embraced death, with the assurance that God was in control. Whatever happened to him was with God's full knowledge and contributed to the fulfillment of His ultimate plan. No, Dana wouldn't be full of doubt and anger at God. But I myself longed for reassurance. I couldn't keep staring into this pit of despair.

Sitting up in bed, I grabbed my Bible from the night stand. *God help me! Give me something to hold onto,* I prayed. Then I remembered Ruth telling me that she had been memorizing Psalm 139 with Dana before his death. Curiously, I flipped to the chapter and began to read. The words poured soothingly down upon my wounds, and an excitement grew in my heart.

"Ruth and Jody," I exclaimed aloud, "listen to these two verses! ' . . . If I dwell in the remotest part of the sea, Even there Thy hand shall lead me, and Thy right hand will lay hold of me' " (vs. 9 NAS).

Ruth smiled knowingly and sat next to me on the bed, her eyes intently scanning the chapter, "Let me read this one," she said, her features alight. " 'Thy eyes have seen my unformed substance; And in Thy book they were all written, The days that were ordained for me, When as yet there was not one of them' " (vs. 16 NAS).

"You know, Renee," Ruth continued, "why don't we go see the man who's keeping our station wagon? Since he led the search party, maybe he can tell us something."

"Yes," Jody agreed. "Dad said what a good man he is. I'd like to speak to him too."

After talking it over with Mom and Dad, all five of us sped off that evening in our rented car toward Eric McCooeye's home. A few miles down the road, we pulled up to a small log cabin nestled among the woods. There in front was our brown Ford station wagon, waiting for us.

A blond, bearded man with rugged skin, toughened by the outdoors, greeted us with a broad smile. As we sat down at an oak table near the kitchen, we lost no time in asking him some of the questions boiling inside us. Ruth was the first to ask what we all were wondering.

"Do you think Dana's body will be recovered?" she asked nervously. Eric sighed.

"Not likely. The ocean's just 100 miles away and the river is 150-200 feet deep. An entire airplane went down once in that river and only two small pieces were ever found." He dropped his eyes to the floor.

"What about life jackets?" Mom questioned. "Do you think he would have survived if he'd been wearing one?"

"No," Eric said gently, shaking his head. After a moment's hesitation, he went on. "I've seen logs start spinning on end there and then get sucked straight down." I swallowed hard as the terror of Dana's final moments became more and more apparent.

I looked at Dad to see his downcast eyes suddenly turn up to the man's face. Even though Dad held a firm faith in God, I knew he still wondered if he'd been negligent in the accident. Eric's words must have eased

Dad's pain.

Eric went on to explain that about six unsuspecting tourists drown every year in the Skeena River. Only the people living in the area realize the tremendous danger that exists.

Mom's eyes brimmed with tears. "Then why doesn't someone put up a warning sign?"

With an understanding nod, Eric said he would see that it was done. But I sensed that underneath my mother's words was something more. Her face was tense, etched with anger and regret that the death of her son could have been prevented. I knew it was still very hard for her not to view the accident as anything more than she saw it—a tragic mistake that could have been avoided.

"Why don't we pray?" Eric suggested.

We bowed our heads and Eric prayed a firm, strong prayer, asking God for grace and peace to surround us. As he finished, my mother looked up and smiled through tear-stained eyes and I glimpsed the tiniest easing of her pain. Dad put his hand on her shoulder reassuringly as we stood up. Then, as Eric handed Dad the keys to our station wagon, we thanked him and made our way to the front door.

While Jody volunteered to drive the rented car, the rest of us headed for the station wagon. I hesitated as I climbed into the back seat with Ruth, fearing some memento of Dana would be there. Of course nothing had been removed since the night of the accident, and glancing behind me, I recoiled in horror to see a corner of the deflated raft—the raft that had borne my brother to his death. I turned my eyes away and crumpled into my seat. As Dad started the car, I stared straight ahead, trying to stem the flow of tears that kept welling in my eyes.

As we pulled up to the motel in the station wagon, I saw Dad reach inside the glove compartment before we all got out. "Ruth, this is for you," he explained gently, handing her a postcard. "Dana hadn't mailed it yet."

Reading it to herself, Ruth fingered the postcard

tenderly. I curiously peered over her shoulder noticing the date—July 2nd, just two days before he died. In the few sentences, Dana encouraged Ruth to continue memorizing Psalm 139. Then, exclaiming what a wonderful trip he was having, he ended with the words, "The Lord is with us for sure."

Ruth's green eyes were moist as she handed the postcard to my mother. Jody and Dad gathered around to look on.

It was starting to drizzle, so I headed for our motel room. Getting ready for bed, I pondered Dana's last comment on that card. *Had the Lord really been with Dana in his final earthly seconds, choosing to take him to his heavenly home?* And if that were true, could I trust a God who did that? Was He really like the Bible says, loving, just and compassionate?

A few minutes later, Jody and Ruth came into the room. Tucking the postcard carefully in her purse, Ruth said softly, "Renee, I'm going back outside for a while."

I nodded, guessing she needed time to be alone with God and her thoughts. "Don't be too long," I cautioned. "It'll be dark soon and it's starting to rain."

With words of assurance, she headed out the door, and Jody and I got into our beds. Glancing at my wristwatch, I realized what time it was. *Ten o'clock!* Just nine days ago at this time, Dad, Dana and Marty would have been rafting down the Skeena River, in the lingering daylight of the Far North. I closed my eyes and pretended I could somehow turn back the clock and erase the events of that dreadful evening.

An hour later I awoke when the door creaked open. Glimpsing Ruth's petite figure in the darkened room, I pulled myself up in bed and switched on the bedside lamp. Her brown curls damp with rain, she tiptoed over to me, taking care not to wake up Jody.

"I wrote down some of my thoughts tonight," Ruth whispered, grasping a small notebook. "It helps if I write out my feelings to God."

Handing me her open notebook, I began reading:

> *As I write this, they were rafting down the river about 10 p.m., July 4th. Oh, God, receive my praise I pray; receive my tears. Thank you for the rain right now. It reminds me of heavenly tears being shed. I love you, Lord Jesus and I loved Dana—only Thou knowest truly how much. I trust in Thee to fill the void. I am your bride. Oh, let me see Thy countenance and hear Thy voice.*

I took a deep breath and let it out. Ruth had such a childlike trust in God! But before I could say anything, she turned the page and explained, "I copied this part from one of Jim Elliot's letters to his wife, Elisabeth. It's exactly what I thought Dana would have wanted to say to me tonight."

I read on:

> *I charge you in the name of our Unfailing Friend, do away with all waverings, bewilderment, and wonder . . . Overcome anything in the confidence of your union with Him, so that contemplating trial, enduring persecution or loneliness, you may know the blessings of 'the joy set before.' We are the sheep of His pasture. Enter into His gates with thanksgiving and into His courts with praise.[3]*

Ruth leaned back against the headboard, still clutching her journal. "I felt really challenged by this, Renee—to praise God despite the difficulties. So I did—right out there, sitting in the rain tonight. I praised God. And then I read Philippians." Grabbing the Bible next to my bed, Ruth began reading aloud: "More than that, I count all things to be loss in view of the surpassing value of knowing Christ Jesus my Lord, for whom I have suffered the loss of all things, and count them but rubbish in order that I may gain Christ" (Phil. 3:8 NAS).

I hugged Ruth and thanked her for the encouragement. She smiled and headed for her luggage on the floor a few feet away. While she got ready for bed, I pulled the covers over me and thought about what she had said. It really did help. It wasn't going to be easy to accept and understand Dana's death. And it was going to be even harder to go through the intense pain of grief. But Paul said someday we would experience such joy that our greatest sufferings would be seen as only light afflictions.

Ruth turned out the light and climbed into the double bed beside Jody. Lying there in the dark, I listened as Ruth's breath measured and became slow like Jody's. Little Ruth had shown the way—more keys to facing this grief. The keys were to praise God and spend time alone in His presence, allowing Him to comfort us. Then we could give that comfort to each other, like Ruth had just done for me. As we resisted the tendency to withdraw into separate walls of despair, we could help each other release our sorrow.

I turned over to make one more attempt at getting to sleep. But a growing apprehension suddenly took shape in thought. Tomorrow we would go to the river. I'd need as much help from God as I could get to face the scene of the accident and Dana's last minutes on earth.

Chapter 9

The Dark River

The old trestle bridge loomed eerily through the morning fog as we drove up. I stepped outside into the dismal morning, wrapping my blue jacket tighter around me to ease the chill. Scarcely noticing the colorful array of wild flowers surrounding me, I stepped onto the river bank and followed the rest of our family. We crossed onto the bridge where, just 10 days earlier, Marty stood making a video of Dana and Dad.

Peering over a splintered wooden rail, I gazed out at the cold green water. For the first time, I could understand why they had gone rafting here in the first place. The river didn't look that bad, so strangely deceiving, seemingly innocent and tranquil, sweeping down river in its glorious progression. Straining to look closer, I edged my body further over the rail. Only under the bridge was there a sign of white water and that was merely a small patch. The uninitiated would never guess it was a deadly whirlpool.

However, as I watched closely, water bubbled to the surface from unseen pressure at the bottom. I stood transfixed as little whirlpools began to form out of the calm, then swiftly became bigger whirlpools as the force downward grew violent. My hope that perhaps Dana was only injured was now shattered as I stared at the downward spirals of water. There would be no miracle. Dana wasn't going to suddenly turn up, recovering in some small back-woods cabin or lying unconscious in some hospital. He was dead and his body was in the depths of this river, or per-haps far out in the Pacific.

As I stood looking at the river's deception, I realized how many times my perspective was off and how different life can appear when you only look on the surface.

For long minutes, my family and I stood on the bridge, our only tangible way of touching Dana. I thought of the loss, the seemingly senseless tragedy that happened right here just days before. Now Dana would never have a chance to graduate. He'd never be a father or go into mis-sions as a doctor as he planned. Had God made a mistake? Were his life and training futile, snuffed out too soon? If success was measured in terms of position or money—or if life was meaningless without leaving behind tangible monuments—or even if success was based on Christian "good works"—the answer would definitely be yes. But then, if God were really all-knowing, all-wise and all-seeing, what was His perspective in all of this? What is the proper length of a man's life in God's eyes? Unlike us, He alone sees the deep currents below the surface of our cir-cumstances.

I pulled my eyes from the water and swept them up across the majestic snow-peaked mountains surrounding us. "Someday, Lord," I whispered, "make sense of all this for me."

I looked down the bridge at my mother, slumped against the rail. A blue scarf framed her tear-stained face as she stared wordlessly for long minutes into the river. Then abruptly, her head drooped down, cupped by one of her hands. I imagined her mother's instinct longed to reach out in protection to save her boy from the swirling waters. But she was too late, powerless to change what had already taken place.

Suddenly a hard verse from the Bible hit me. Didn't it say in Isaiah 43:2, "When you pass through the waters, I will be with you; And through the rivers, they will not overflow you?" (NAS) So what about Dana? He was a child of God. *Why did God allow the waters to overflow him?*

Although my heart was in anguish, I had to cling to God's promise to be with us, even though I didn't understand. The rivers and the storms of life may test us, but God did not promise to deliver us from them. Certainly He could have chosen to keep us from this tragedy and suffering. Why He chose not to, I didn't know. I only knew we had the promise of His presence in the face of life's worst crises, and the promise that He would never leave us. In Dana's case, he had gone through the testing waters of life only to be led into new life with God for all eternity.

I drew a long breath, then spotted Ruth hunched over at the river's edge, picking wild flowers. I darted over to see what she was up to. Her body straightened as she pulled from her bouquet one yellow daisy with a rather long stem.

Cradling the small blossom carefully between her fingers, Ruth said quietly, "This daisy reminds me of a verse in Isaiah, 'For He grew up before Him like a tender shoot.' " Her hazy eyes focused on its stem as she ran her fingers along it. "It's as though Dana was never really mine, but God's to do with as He wished."

Placing my arm around Ruth, I gave her a gentle squeeze. Then stooping down, I began gathering my own assortment of red, purple and yellow flowers. Soon, Mom, Dad and Jody came over and Ruth suggested that we all get flowers to throw into the river as a memorial to Dana.

A few minutes later we stood on the bridge, clutching our flowers and gazing down over the spot of Dana's home-going. Into my mind came an old hymn, written a century earlier by a man who had lost his four daughters to a storm at sea. He penned a well-known hymn as he later sailed over the very spot of their accident, and now its familiar strains came out of my lips.

When peace like a river attendeth my way....

Soon the others joined me and, surrounded by the wild beauty of Canada, we sang through our tears:

> When sorrows like sea billows roll—
> Whatever my lot Thou hast taught me to say
> It is well, it is well with my soul.[4]

Still tremendous sorrow was buried in our hearts, for although the grace of God was sufficient, it was not anesthetic. Had God consulted us before His angels took Dana to heaven, we would have pleaded, "Please, Lord, don't take him! We love him too much and want him here with us!"

But though we grieved, I clung to the scripture saying we do not grieve as those who have no hope. I wanted to hold onto the words I had read in a book called *Not By Accident:* "... the circumstances that surround an accident are insignificant to a child of God, but the God who surrounds the circumstances is infinite."

Dad, with his quiet strength and faith, led us in prayer, speaking out his trust that God loved us and would help us even now. Then we all softly joined in the tune of "How Great Thou Art" until our voices trailed off in the crisp mountain air. As we finished singing, I recalled a few words Dana had shared with me from Jim Elliot's journals:

> Lord, make my way prosperous, not that I
> achieve high station but that my life may be
> an exhibit to the value of knowing God.[5]

Then we flung the flowers from the bridge, watching as the confetti of colored blooms floated down stream. As we sadly made our way off the bridge to begin our long journey back to California, all I wanted was to put Hazelton and this dark river behind me. But at the same time, I wondered how we would cope when we returned to the routine of everyday living. As it turned out, I'd have little chance to find out for quite a while.

The Taft family, 1963
Front Row — Renee, Dorothy, Dana, Keith, Jody
Back Row — Marty

Dana and Jody, 1975

Ruth and Dana on their wedding day,
June 20, 1981.

Marty congratulating Dana after the wedding.

Dana,
June 26, 1984

My friend, Rhonda Robson Bell
1981

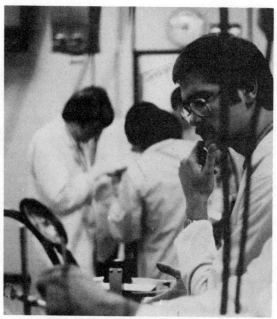

Dana in medical school.

My mother, Dorothy, on the bridge (above and below left), overlooking the spot of her son's last minutes on earth.

My parents, Keith and Dorothy, in Hazelton, Canada — July 1984.

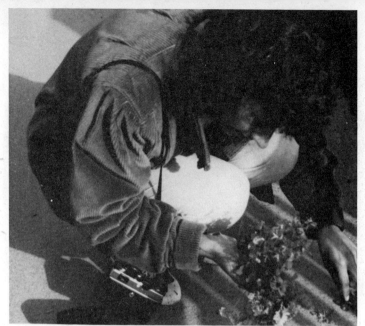

Ruth on the bridge, collecting wild flowers.

My father, Keith, with Ruth, minutes before
throwing their flowers from the bridge.

Renee, on the bridge, gazing at her
bouquet of wild flowers.

Renee, throwing flowers from the bridge.

Chapter 10

Bitter or Better

We had been up before dawn, speeding through Oregon towards California on the last leg of our 2,000 mile journey. I yawned and rubbed my eyes. Even after several hours on the road I was still trying to wake up. Dad peered over the steering wheel, searching for a place to have a late breakfast. Jody had flown back to Dallas from Canada, so I stretched out across the extra space available. Ruth sat quietly on the other side of the back seat with her Bible opened to Psalm 139, memorizing her verse for that day, as she and Dana had agreed.

For all of us, the pain of grief was still so intense, that I wondered if we could have endured it without the daily strength and comfort of the scriptures. It seemed almost like the Book of Psalms had been written just for us. We especially identified with King David in Psalm 31:9, and it also became our prayer: "Be gracious to me, O Lord, for I am in distress; My eye is wasted from grief, my soul and my body also."

Other scriptures also continually reassured us: " . . . I will turn their mourning into joy, I will comfort them, and give them gladness for sorrow . . ."(Jer. 31:13). Time and again, the Word of God became the oil that soothed our wounded hearts. We chose to believe the truths we were reading, and not go by our feelings. God said He was near to the brokenhearted and as we laid bare our broken hearts before Him, we found that He was indeed near.

Ruth also found renewed hope as she diligently searched the scriptures. God specifically promises in His Word to look after widows and now Ruth was in that special category. Without a husband, and perhaps never becoming a wife again or a mother, Ruth's life was altered tremendously. But she claimed God's promise for herself in Jeremiah 29:11: " 'For I know the plans I have for you,' says the Lord, 'plans for welfare and not for evil to give you a future and a hope.' "

Soon Dad veered the car off the highway and pulled up to a restaurant. I unfolded out of the back seat and stiffly walked inside as a waitress ushered us toward a booth. I passed by a dark-haired woman about my age who stared at me, when she abruptly spoke. "Renee?"

"Yes?" I answered, trying to place her face. Then it hit me. She had been my best friend in high school!

"Gayle! What a surprise!" I hadn't seen her since we'd graduated 11 years earlier.

I started to tell her about our loss of Dana when something struck deep. When Gayle herself was in eighth grade, her own mother had drowned in their back yard swimming pool.

Now 16 years later, I could finally identify with the grief she must have experienced. "I know all about that," Gayle whispered sadly, her deep brown eyes portraying a real link of understanding.

That day became yet another step to healing. Now I knew that with any suffering we go through, we can have greater compassion toward others. We become more sensitive and not so quick to judge or give our "if-that-were-me" analysis to suffering people. And as we look to God for the comfort we need in our sorrow, we can identify with the Apostle Paul who wrote: "Blessed be the God and Father of our Lord Jesus Christ, the Father of mercies and

God of all comfort, who comforts us in all our affliction, so that we may be able to comfort those who are in any affliction, with the comfort with which we ourselves are comforted by God" (II Cor. 1:3-4).

But as I said goodbye to Gayle to rejoin my family, the idea that I could grow and help others from my sorrow suddenly annoyed me. *What do I care about other people?* Right now I hurt too much to focus on anyone else's misery. Besides, this wasn't the way I wanted to help others more effectively. I wanted to shout out loud, "Forget it! Just give me back my brother!"

On July 18th, we pulled into the driveway of our home in Sunnyvale, California. Picking up the pieces of our routine, it was still hard to believe Dana was really gone. But whenever I entered our living room in the next few days, I couldn't escape the truth. There before me, in boxes and strewn across the carpet, lay Dana's medical books, his favorite pillow, the knapsack he was so proud of—all gathered from the station wagon. Seeing each item sent shock waves of nausea through me.

It was especially hard for Ruth. As I sat at the kitchen table one day, I watched Ruth pausing over a box in our living room. Suddenly, her head dropped and her body went limp. As I approached, I could understand as I peered down. There was Dana's stethoscope lying at the bottom.

"He wore it every day in medical school," Ruth whispered, trying to stifle a cry. All I could do was nod knowingly and hurt with her.

I knew the stethoscope brought a landslide of memories for Ruth—memories that were now unbelievably filled with sorrow. She later penned the following words in her journal:

> *Every day the reality sinks in a little more. I feel so numb because of it! How I miss him—his beautiful, sensitive eyes, the conversations we had so often, his hugs, but*

*mostly his spirit—I long to be able to talk
with him about the Lord.*

*It has been two weeks exactly since Dana's
death. It seems like an eternity!! Parts of me
still can't believe it has really happened. I expect to have him call or see him in a few
weeks but when I think of all our belongings
and what I should do with them, it grips my
heart like a vise and the grief overwhelms me.
Help me, Jesus, to cope with what each day
brings.*

As the days progressed, Dana continued to consume
our waking thoughts as we struggled through the motions
of our ongoing lives. How I wish I had known what to expect. But we were traveling an uncharted course.

I was especially surprised to find how much energy it
took to do the ordinary, mundane duties of everyday life.
It was difficult, if not impossible, to go at our normal pace.
I never knew how apathy and listlessness would sap our
strength. It took all the energy we could muster just to get
up in the morning, make the bed, get dressed and do the
dishes. Everything seemed so unimportant now. What difference did it make if the bed got made or the dishes were
washed? Who cared?

But in those days I learned another important step
toward healing. First, since the emotions of grief exhausted
me, I learned not to put unrealistic expectations upon
myself. I began to accept the fact that I was not as ener-
getic and productive as before. At the same time, I found
that prolonged inactivity only intensified my depression
and left me preoccupied with sad thoughts, so I forced
myself to seek some outlets. Daily I immersed myself in
writing letters, talking out my feelings with others,
memorizing scripture and spending time with God, not to
mention at least some housework, no matter how insignificant it now seemed. And slowly, though progress often

seemed at a standstill, the gnawing ache inside began to lessen.

My mother still found it hard to sleep, and often when sleep did come, she awoke with nightmares. One morning, shortly after we arrived home, I awoke very early and went to the kitchen to get a drink of water. There sat Mom, bent over the table with a pen in her hand, writing intently. As I moved closer she glanced up with a surprised look. I could tell by her red eyes and swollen face that it was another bad night.

I placed my arm around her shoulder. "What's wrong, Mom?"

A storm of tears rushed down her face. "Oh," she groaned, "I dreamed I threw Dana a rope." Deep sobs shook her as she cupped her hand over her face. "I woke myself up yelling, 'Hang on! Hang on to the raft!' "

Pulling a chair up next to her, I rubbed Mom's shoulder as she continued to cry. Then, pushing a white paper in front of me, she stammered, "I . . . I've been writing down my feelings. It helps some."

Picking up the tear-stained paper, I saw these neatly-penned words:

> *Another bad night with bad images going through my mind. Trying to pray. Feels like my insides are being torn apart and the pain at times seems unbearable. Will the Lord hear my cries? Will there ever be joy again? Why, oh why, Lord? I have so many regrets—wish I could change things. I need to dwell on scripture and try to be more positive. But right now I think, "Lord, you have a heaven full of treasures. Couldn't you have waited to exercise your claim on Dana?"*

Putting the letter down, I reached my arms around her and hugged her tight. Then, as Mom wiped her eyes on the hem of her robe, I saw again how writing helped us release some of the inner struggles with anger, remorse and questioning. Instead of denying her loss, as we all did in our initial reactions, Mom was beginning to face it. And so, as we slowly made our way down the hall to our bedrooms, I silently prayed, *God, give us nights of peaceful, healing sleep again.*

But there were still more lessons to learn before we'd see the answer to that prayer.

Chapter 11

Jesus, Weep With Me

Before long, Ruth accepted my parents' invitation to leave Tulsa and live with our family in California. Her mother and I both offered to fly out with Ruth and help sort through she and Dana's possessions. Marty and my parents would also join us in a few days to help, and though it wasn't the easiest trip, it would be one more step toward healing.

It was July 21st as Ruth, her mother and I first stepped into the apartment Ruth and Dana had shared in Tulsa, Oklahoma. Scanning the living room, a fresh wave of grief seared me as my eyes fell on a framed picture of Dana with a broad, white smile. Over on a coffee table lay his old leather-covered Bible which he always carried tucked under his arm. Once precious memories, they were now horrible reminders of the magnitude of our loss. Ruth's composure melted as she stared at their wedding picture which hung nearby. Her head fell in despair.

"I need to be alone for a while," Ruth whispered, escaping to her bedroom around the corner.

Mrs. Herbert and I went into the kitchen and sat down at the small white table. There on the wall behind us were yet more pictures—Dana smiling from beneath a helmet on a motorcycle; Dana studying on his favorite sofa. Trembling inside, I recoiled. Every small memory now became unbearably filled with sorrow.

After 45 minutes of waiting with Mrs. Herbert, I knocked on Ruth's bedroom door to see if she was okay. Opening it cautiously, I saw Ruth sitting on the edge of the waterbed, her eyes staring blankly at the floor. As I sat down beside her, tears sprang from her eyes. "Everything's such a shock," she sobbed. "I feel so alone."

Putting my arm around Ruth, I sat with her in silence for several minutes. Finally, not knowing what to say, I prayed God would somehow help us survive. Again, his answer was only minutes away.

Ruth stood up unsteadily, explaining that she was going outside to get the mail. Her mom and I were unpacking our few belongings in the living room, when Ruth came bounding back with a glint in her eyes. She looked like a different person than the girl I'd just prayed with. In one of her hands was an opened letter.

"While I was in the bedroom," she explained breathlessly, "I prayed I could talk with another widow." She shoved the open letter into my hand. "Look, here's my answered prayer!"

The woman wrote that she had worked a short time with Dana at the hospital. Her own husband had died just two years ago in a work-related accident when she was only 24. The woman asked if she and Ruth, whom she'd never met, could get together and talk.

The answer had come right when Ruth needed it the most and she was greatly encouraged. It was a reminder to all of us that God cared about our smallest need. For all the pain we felt, we were powerfully learning how close our Heavenly Father is when we walk through the deepest, darkest valleys of our lives.

But our first night's sleep in the seemingly hollow apartment proved to be another testing time for Ruth, as she later shared in her journal:

> *I slept well but with dreams, the last being
> able to talk with Dana a bit. When I awoke*

> *the finality of it all hit me. He isn't in another*
> *room, or at the hospital, or in California get-*
> *ting ready to start his clerkships. Oh, Jesus,*
> *you wept with Mary and Martha over*
> *Lazarus. Will you weep with me? I ask for*
> *your comfort. The ache in my heart is so*
> *great. I feel no relief from it. Father, I fear I*
> *will grow numb and cold because of the pain.*
> *Make me have a heart like David's, always*
> *turned towards Thee even in shame and*
> *great pain.*

The next morning three of Dana's friends volunteered to help us pack his books. As we worked, one stopped and looked up at me with a pile of books in his hands.

"Renee . . . " he hesitated. "I don't know if this will help but . . . you know I was concerned that Dana might be taking his prayer and Bible study too far in school. I told him he could be a top medical student if he'd stop having his 'mega quiet times.' " He smiled a little.

"What did Dana say?"

"Dana said his relationship with God was more important, even if he failed his classes." Then, gazing down at one of Dana's textbooks, he added sheepishly, "I'm glad he didn't take my advice."

I smiled at him, glad he'd told me the little story. I too was thankful Dana had made the decision he did, especially since his medical training wouldn't be put to use now.

Instead of Dana going overseas himself, we began packing up his text books to send to doctors who worked on board a missionary ship. But as I stared at the boxes being rapidly filled with those precious volumes, I fought the desire to scream, *Stop! Don't take them away!* I didn't want Dana's books given to other doctors to use. They were Dana's. They belonged to him. He had spent hundreds of hours studying them. He could have used those books to heal countless of lives.

In anguish, I stared at the almost empty bookcase. It

was as though a surgeon's knife had cut open a wound in me that would never heal. With every book that was packed, a piece of me—the piece that Dana once had filled— seemed to be sliced and ripped away.

As the last few books were swept away and put into boxes, Ruth appeared calmly from the bedroom, holding a load of Dana's clothes. His friends sorted through them, taking what they liked and the rest would go to others. I turned away, unable to bear seeing the last fragments of Dana's life disappear.

That evening, sleep avoided me as I lay on the living room floor beside Mrs. Herbert. At least my brother, Marty, and my parents would be arriving tomorrow. That would help. I hadn't realized before I walked into that empty apartment the pain that this step would require. Even in the darkened living room, I could still make out the black shape of that empty bookshelf, stripped of my brother's books.

I turned away, burrowing myself under the covers, muffling my sobs so I wouldn't wake Ruth's mom. The deep, unspeakable loss felt like a crushing weight on my chest and waves of nausea swept over me. I'd heard it said that the tears of God's people on earth were made into perfume in heaven—and I knew at least tonight, heaven would be having plenty of perfume.

Chapter 12

Making Mistakes

Why do we so zealously train and plan for life's great events and fail to learn how to walk through grieving before it is upon us? We have seminars for young marrieds, classes for childbirth—every stage of life receives attention, but we blunder into facing life's greatest challenges with so little preparation.

That was the reason, I suppose, that we didn't know what we were all doing wrong at this point. First, we rushed the business of getting rid of Dana's things, perhaps causing Ruth to suffer the most. Of course my parents and my brother, Marty, had also arrived in Tulsa, and we wanted to help move Ruth out to California as soon as possible. But Ruth was forced to quickly sift through their possessions, and then to add to her stress, she reported to her work each day as a lab technician. Conscientious Ruth, even in her bereavement, was trying to give her employer at least two weeks' notice before resignation.

While Ruth was at work each day, Marty and Dad tried to sell two trucks that Dana had owned. Meanwhile, my mother and Mrs. Herbert worked in the apartment, making tough decisions about what to do with Dana's belongings. But Ruth tended to protest any decision that was made without her and grew increasingly edgy. She found it painful to part with anything and no amount of pushing or practical advice would budge her. As a result,

we spent our days mostly waiting for Ruth to get home
from work, cleaning cupboards, or finding other little odds
and ends that needed to be done.

I suppose we might have stumbled on, unknowingly
increasing Ruth's pain if it hadn't been for the matter of
the dresser.

Ruth advertised several pieces of furniture for sale,
and one day while she was at work, my mother sold the
dresser Ruth had shared with Dana. Just as Mom was
about to empty its contents, she decided to call Ruth and
see if she would mind. Mom didn't know she was bringing
back the reality of Dana's death for Ruth by rushing the
sale along, but complied with Ruth's request to wait until
she got home. Only later did we learn of Ruth's feelings as
she recorded them in her journal:

> *God, another blow! Can I stand it? Help me
> survive, Lord. Dana's mom just called and
> said she had sold the dresser and asked if it
> could be emptied so that she could give it to
> the new owner. Oh, Lord, how precious are
> Dana's things in that one drawer that I
> wanted to pack carefully away and all my
> clothes in the other. Can people understand
> what I'm going through? Help me to convey
> it in a gracious way. Everything is shocking to
> me. Each sale of our things rings with the
> finality of Dana's death!!*

We didn't know it was so unwise to rush Ruth into
selling treasured memories of her husband. It only caused
her more pain, robbing her of the time she needed to
gradually adjust and accept her loss. Trying to make her be
"practical" and realize her things were now useless was not
necessarily practical in helping her regain emotional well-
being. We didn't know what a mistake we were making.

The next day, as my family and I were on a tour of the
hospital—the same tour that Dana had given me when I

visited him—I felt that familiar cutting inside the pit of my stomach. Questions kept racing through my head as I passed medical students in their white overcoats. Why wasn't my brother here? Hadn't Dana's professors said what a fine doctor he would be? Hadn't Dana's fellow students told us how godly he was? Then, why *my* brother?

Certainly God could have protected Dana, as He did for Daniel in the Lion's den, and Moses in the Red Sea and others I had read about in the Bible. But then again, why did God lift His hand of protection from Stephen when he was being stoned to death or from 10 of Jesus' 12 disciples? Why did God seem to protect some and not others?

As I shuffled down a long corridor, staring straight ahead, while fighting to control my pent up emotions, I just wasn't sure of anything any more. Did God let good, young people die to inspire us by their lives, so we will redeem the time ourselves and live more fully for Him? Or could it be that God wants us to follow Him not for the blessings we receive but because He exists and is worthy of our very lives?

All of a sudden, I realized I had stumbled onto another major truth in this dark valley—trust. What is trust anyway? We say we trust God, but that only is true if we don't have all the answers. Suddenly, I knew my faith would have to operate in the dark for now, putting into action the real meaning of trust. Although my emotions were unglued, I had to hang on to what I knew of God through the Bible and my own relationship with Him. Perhaps some day I would see His perspective on what was accomplished by "every grain of wheat which falls into the earth and dies" (John 12:24). Until then, all I could understand was that His still, small voice seemed to whisper in my heart, *Just trust me.*

I glanced at my mother walking beside me in the corridor, teary-eyed and biting her lower lip. Her real heartache was evident. Ruth, too, was silent, but Dad and Marty carried on bravely, politely questioning our guide about hospital procedures—matters totally unimportant to me now that Dana was gone. The guide patiently answered the questions, but the words droned in the background of my inner struggle as every step through those halls cut deeper into my heart.

Then Mom voiced what we all felt. "Dana would have made a fine doctor," she said shaking her head.

While Mom's pain echoed my own, the truth of her words knived me. And I don't think I could've taken another step without Ruth's immediate answer, "Mom, the other students may get their degrees, but I believe Dana got the better deal!"

Mom's eyebrows raised in surprise as she let out a little laugh, and a ray of hope descended upon her clouded face for the first time. For Ruth had spoken the reality for any Christian who goes to be with Christ. Didn't the Apostle Paul say in Philippians that "to live is Christ, and to die is gain"? So no matter how great the life or prospective future seems to be here on earth, doesn't any Christian who dies really get "the better deal"?

As we finished our tour through the hospital, we met with many of Dana's classmates at a spaghetti dinner at one student's apartment. An atmosphere of warmth and lightheartedness pervaded as Marty shared many of the experiences that he had with Dana while growing up.

Ruth and my father tried to be cheerful but my mother, fatigued and weary-eyed, remained untypically quiet. At the end of the meeting, we all joined hands and one student fervently prayed, "Lord, let peace—that soothing, restful, comforting peace of God—surround this family."

As he continued, my mother began to sob. Ever since Dana died, Mom had been tormented with nightmares of unsuccessfully trying to rescue Dana, and hadn't had one peaceful night. And as we all went home that evening, I wondered if she'd ever experience real peace again.

But the next morning, I was surprised to see no bags of fatigue under my mother's eyes at breakfast. "God answered that student's prayer!" she announced. "I slept soundly all night!"

Yes, answered prayers had been coming fast and steady for us, and we thanked God for the ways He was meeting our needs. More and more He'd been guiding us on the path through grief, and we would know the grace and comfort of God in even greater ways in the days ahead. For soon we'd all be heading back to California, and we couldn't yet perceive how often grief would catch us unaware, like a thief in the night.

PART III

THE FINAL FAREWELL

"Oh, death, where is thy sting? O grave, where is thy victory?" (I Cor. 15:55 KJV)

Chapter 13

Found

Ruth and I sat spellbound in the nearly bare apartment in Tulsa, watching the television screen before us. The flags, a rainbow of ascending balloons and finally the torch runner's arrival signaled the opening ceremonies for the 1984 summer Olympic games in Los Angeles, California. It was spectacular.

After three weeks of grieving, it was a welcome relief from the anguish we still bore in our hearts. The others had gone onto Dallas, visiting my sister and her husband for a couple days, and soon, all of us would head back for California. I couldn't wait to go home and put the painful memories of this city far behind me. Only two more days in Tulsa and our nightmare would be over.

The ringing of the phone interrupted our show. Reluctantly, I picked up the phone, my eyes still focused on the Olympics.

"Hello?" I said nonchalantly.

"Hello, Renee. Is Ruth there?" It was Dad. But why was his voice so strangely subdued?

"Dad, is something wrong?"

He paused as if not wanting to explain. *What else could have happened?* After all, nothing could be any worse than what we'd already gone through.

"Well," he explained, his voice lowering even more, "They . . . they found Dana's body."

The words felt like a bullet, ripping through my body and lodging in the center of my chest. I fell limply into a chair. "Oh, no! No!" I gasped, still clutching the phone. My mind and emotions rose in protest, refusing to accept this final proof of my brother's death. I groaned, then raised my head to the sound of Ruth's footsteps coming toward me.

"They found Dana's body, didn't they?" she asked resolutely.

Nodding numbly, I handed Ruth the phone, amazed at her calm exterior. Wanting to escape, I ran into the living room, crumbled into the sofa and hid my face in my hands.

A few minutes later, Ruth quietly came and sat next to me, filling me in on the details. I caught a little steadiness from her as she explained that Dana's body had been found 60 miles downstream from where the raft had first tipped over. The coroner had made positive identification with the dental charts we had sent.

"Mom got on the phone," Ruth continued sadly. "She was sobbing but said she'd been praying all along that Dana would be found. She said she needed the finality."

Ruth told me she wanted to fly back to Canada to bury Dana in Hazelton, but Mom wanted to bury Dana in the United States.

"She said she needed him closer because his little bones were formed in her," Ruth said, shaking her head. "I guess it's hard for me to understand because I've never been a mother."

Then Ruth and I sat and prayed together, asking God for strength and the wisdom to know where Dana should be buried. My mother had suggested Minnesota, where Mom grew up, or perhaps California—but for some reason, both places seemed unsuitable to Ruth.

But as we finished praying, Ruth smiled a little. "Dana always loved Montana—especially the thunderstorms," she added. "And he often talked about Glacier National Park, and how beautiful it is."

Memories of the years I'd spent with my family, camping and hiking around the park, suddenly came racing back. Dana was born in Montana and lived the first several years of his life there. My father had been raised near Glacier National Park in Cut Bank, and his parents still lived there. They even had a family burial plot.

With a resolute toss of her small head, Ruth declared, "Montana! Do you think Mom would agree?"

I shrugged. We'd have to see. But first, Ruth had another matter to settle. She had to inform her boss of another needed absence to take care of her husband's burial. As she explained the situation to him on the phone, I couldn't help over hearing her apologetic tone. She needed to leave immediately, to go and bury her husband.

"I'm sorry, I know it's an inconvenience for you," she was saying. "I'll try to be back as soon as possible."

"What's wrong?" I snapped. By now my anger was rising.

"He said my priorities should be with my job." Ruth sighed dismally. I couldn't believe her employer had actually tried to make her feel guilty, with all she was going through.

"Ruth, you need to quit—for good!" I stormed. "I don't care if your employer understands or not!"

Trying to calm myself over her employer's insensitivity, I tried to explain that Ruth's priorities at this time were with herself and her family. She badly needed to give herself some time, and to continue working would only put a further load on her, not to mention the rest of us. We still had packing to do and needed to bury Dana immediately.

Ruth nodded quietly in agreement, her face showing the first signs of real strain. She promised to call her employer back and tell him she was leaving Tulsa for good.

Of course when someone has major surgery, no one expects them to be back on the job right away, maintaining the same pace or productivity level. They're encouraged to take it easy and get well. Everyone knows they need time to heal.

But when someone has had a major personal loss, like a death in the family, society seems to expect immediate, quick recovery. The one who bravely continues on, taking it "well," and acting as if nothing has happened, so often is given praise. People somehow forget that an emotional wound also takes time to heal—perhaps even longer than a physical injury might require.

I also felt the strain of the past few days. At least Marty and my parents would come back tomorrow morning to help again. Then I could get away from this grim apartment. All I wanted was to escape the pain of Tulsa and prepare as best I could for the upcoming graveside service.

Since the remaining items to be packed were only for Ruth to sort through, I would be flying out to Dallas the next morning to spend some time with my sister, Jody, and her husband, Scott. But I was going with mixed feelings, for Dallas was the home of Rhonda's parents—Rhonda, who had been killed just four months ago. And I hadn't gone to her funeral. Would the memories of Rhonda be too much for me to cope with right now? Would I be able to be a comfort to her parents if I saw them?

I would soon find out. But in the meantime, I was eager to leave behind a city that had only given me unforgettable sorrow.

Chapter 14

Faced With Reality

I knocked cautiously on the front door of the cozy brick home of Rhonda's parents, the Robsons. A familiar sight, the home reminded me of so many fun weekends spent there during college. Now the Texas noonday sun beat down fiercely as I tried to steady myself to greet Rhonda's mother. *What would I say to her?*

Mrs. Robson opened the door with a gust of refreshing air conditioning and threw her arms around me, easing my fears a bit. Despite the suffering she'd been through, Mrs. Robson still looked young for her 50's, her dark brown hair neatly in place and her red dress nicely showing off her trim figure. But after our warm embrace, I saw the same sad eyes on her face that were now all too familiar in my family these days.

Mrs. Robson ushered me inside, but as we walked toward the kitchen I froze in my tracks. There, on the living room wall, was a huge picture of Rhonda in her wedding gown.

Tears welled up in my eyes as I moved closer. Rhonda stood seriously in her long, white satin gown, with silky blonde hair flowing softly to her shoulders from beneath a veil. Vividly, her china blue eyes peered at me. It was hard to believe she wasn't still alive!

Lingering over the photograph as Mrs. Robson stood with me, I gazed into Rhonda's eyes. "Oh, Rhonda," I groaned. And as I finally turned away, everything in me yearned to bring her back.

Mrs. Robson and I then sat at the round dining room table with several albums of photographs spread out. Carefully I inspected each picture of Rhonda growing up, and then on to her wedding pictures. Could it have only been two years ago that I received the glowing reports of Rhonda's wedding?

Next Mrs. Robson took out a bundle of letters and papers written by her daughter. All of them—even hastily jotted notes—were savored by the two of us. Rhonda's mother let her tears flow freely as we shared fond memories of a special girl. Then she handed me a letter Rhonda had written to the Lord just one year ago—eight months before her death. My eyes fell on these words on the parchment-like paper:

> I, Rhonda Bell, today covenant with You, Lord God—Father, Son, Holy Spirit—to love You all the days of my life.

> You are my Lord. I commit all that I am, have or will have to You irrevocably. In committing myself—all my hopes, dreams and desires—I ask You to remember Your merciful nature; please be kind and gentle.

> This day, all of me, irrevocably, becomes Yours. It will be my joy to wake up each day with thoughts of how to please You. But give me the will also; create in me steadfastness and a deep unflinching trust. Reveal Yourself to me and be my beloved friend.

> I commit to You the following desires:

> — a ministry, anointed by You

—a godly husband to love me
—an education—understanding wisdom
—a skill which can be employed in your service

Most of all, I desire to know You intimately
and to walk with You like Daniel, Abraham,
Enoch, Joseph . . . even like Jesus.

As I re-folded the paper neatly, I realized that God
had answered the desires of Rhonda's heart. He had given
her a wonderful husband and she had just finished her college degree in biblical studies. And certainly, like Dana,
Rhonda must have found that death had unlocked the
gateway to a more intimate relationship with God than is
possible here on earth.

But why, just when Rhonda's desires were fulfilled
and she could employ her gifts in His service, had she been
taken from this earth? My mind went back to Ruth as she
handed me that blossom beside the river. These two,
Rhonda and Dana, for some reason, God had plucked out.

Before I had a chance for more reflection, Mrs. Robson handed me a picture. I shrank in horror at the sight.
There, in a white casket lay Rhonda, clothed in a blue silk
dress; beside her was a perfectly formed baby boy. I swallowed hard. Her mom explained she had kept the picture
to remember how beautiful the baby was. But I could only
tremble inside as I came face to face with this horrible,
stark reality. And the burial of my own brother was just
days away! At least, I tried to reassure myself, I wouldn't
have to view his body.

Rhonda's mother prayed for me as I sat numbly at the
table, but the sorrow in my heart made it hard to concentrate. Opening my eyes at the end of the prayer, I saw
the same anguish in Mrs. Robson's red-rimmed eyes, and I
gave her a hug goodbye. I was grateful to have someone
who could identify with me in my pain, but as I headed out
the door I wondered if I'd ever be free from the thick web
of despair entangling me.

Several hours later, I lay on Jody and Scott's couch trying unsuccessfully to sleep in their living room. Their understanding and willingness to listen to me over dinner had been a great comfort, but there was something I still needed to learn. A stage of grief had yet to be encountered—the stage of guilt. And tonight, as I thought back to a painful time in Dana's life, my mind festered with feelings of remorse.

Eight years earlier, when Dana had just turned 18, I encouraged him to join a Christian organization that ended up hurting him. After several months of working with them full-time, he had left bitter over the injustice he felt he'd received.

Dana had greatly struggled over the next year, until he finally learned to forgive the ones who hurt him. As a result, Dana gained more compassion and understanding when others suffered, and had even told me he wanted to guard against his own pride and critical attitudes.

But now, as I reflected back on this painful time in Dana's life, I couldn't seem to focus on the good that came out of it. Now all I could remember was Dana's pain—I was sure it had been all my fault. I was the one who encouraged him to join that group in the first place. I had been directly responsible for a year of misery in his life, and I was full of remorse.

Submerged in more pain and grief, I lost all ability to see it in perspective. Now my human mistake sprang into criminal-sized proportions. Guilt loomed huge and irrational inside me. And too, I felt anger—because with the discovery of Dana's body, I could no longer deny my loss. I felt angry at anyone and everyone who had caused Dana the slightest amount of hardship during his short stay on earth.

Engulfed by a black fog from which I could not escape, scene after scene of Rhonda and Dana in their coffins flashed before me. I lay paralyzed on the couch, gripped with fear as I was hit head on with the reminder that two people I deeply loved were no longer here on earth. Earlier that day, one of my friends had tried to cheer me up by exhorting me to "just think how happy they must be in heaven." But that didn't help me now. I was mourning the fact that my dear ones were gone from my side! Their being in heaven did not console me. Besides, if heaven has no concept of time as we know it, Rhonda and Dana would be there for eternity anyway. So why would God have minded if they stuck around here on on earth for another 50 years or so?

Chapter 15

Joy Out of Nowhere

I sat stooped at the edge of my hotel bed again, trying to concentrate on the Olympic games on TV—anything to crowd out my nagging fears. After two long days of tense travel, my parents and I still had another day to go in Ruth's small Tercel before we would arrive in Cut Bank for Dana's burial. We all agreed it was the right place, and my dad said there was even room next to Madonna Gail. I would never forget the story of my aunt, who as a little girl had been killed in the school gym by the basketball board. And now, on August 4th, Dana would be buried beside her—exactly one month since his death.

Meanwhile, Marty had flown back home to California to be back on the job and reunited with his wife and children. But in the small case he carried on the plane was special cargo—Dana's pet mouse. "Joey" was not just another white rodent but a small piece of the memories Ruth could still cherish and cling to—a most prized and irreplaceable possession, representing part of the life she and Dana once shared.

Ruth, who stayed behind in Tulsa while a marker was made for the grave, would fly into Cut Bank tomorrow. She told us on the phone that the craftsman was enlarging the cross and dove pattern on Dana's wedding ring, engraving it between the dates 1958-1984. Ruth's ring also bore a cross, always signifying to her the availability of their lives and marriage for God to use as He chose.

Sitting there in the hotel room, I thought of that cross, and how much the love of each person was helping us to shoulder our own individual crosses now. Just to survive, we had to risk reaching out for the support of others. A little motto Ruth had found summed it up so well: "When sharing joy with a friend, it is doubled. When sharing grief with a friend it is divided" (source unknown).

Now in another nameless motel room, I sat staring at the Olympic games, absently watching the American men's gymnastic team win their gold medals. Tears of joy formed in many of the athletes' eyes, a triumphant moment for both them and our country, but nothing seemed to touch me.

As I looked away, the motel wall and furnishings all seemed to be gray. Nothing about the Olympics enthused me. What did it matter? My brother was dead. And although none of us would be viewing his body, I would have to face his coffin in just a few hours.

I turned to the screen to see the figures play out the drama of athletic victory. As they raised the American flag, the national anthem's familiar strains were building—but the music didn't stir me. Instead, it was just one more reminder that life was going on without Dana, undisturbed—not even slowing down.

Dana would've been so interested in these Olympics, I thought. But never again would I enjoy sharing the events and interests with Dana like we once had. Brokenhearted, I fell back on my pillow and quietly began to cry.

But then the most unusual thing happened out of nowhere. There, in the depths of my sorrow, a peace unexpectedly invaded, lifting me above my pain and out of the web of despair entangling me. The weight just fell off my shoulders and the guilt and emptiness disappeared! Slowly, a growing realization came that what I had just seen on television was nothing in comparison to the joy that will be ours in seeing Jesus for the first time!

My tear-stained eyes opened wide in astonishment as joy literally flooded me in that motel room. For the next few moments, I was lifted out of my own grief and given a grasp of the greater honor we would each receive as we reigned with Christ. And even though I knew tremendous sorrow still awaited me in not having Dana here on earth, at that moment the Lord enabled me to rejoice in the joy that must now be Dana's. *He was receiving his gold!*

I drifted into a deep sleep, enveloped in the peace of God. Some day Jesus would wipe away all tears from my eyes forever and I would share in the same joy that Dana had.

Chapter 16

In My Father's House

My parents and I arrived in Cut Bank the next morning and we found our way to the mortuary. The August heat beat down relentlessly as I stepped out of the small car, tightly holding my Bible. I noticed others of my family also clutched their Bibles, as if trying to somehow be prepared for what we were about to see. Ruth, an aunt and uncle, and my grandparents were already waiting on the pillared porch, beside the heavy front door of the funeral home. The last thing I wanted to do was go inside that door.

Dismally, I viewed our surroundings. Cut Bank is a small town set high in the plains of northwest Montana, just 50 miles from the Canadian border. Off in the distance, I saw the outline of the Rockies and Glacier National Park. Memories of family trips in happier childhood days came rushing back. Nothing had changed much now, except for the reason for our visit.

Ruth had been here hours before us, choosing Dana's coffin and settling other arrangements. Now she came to the edge of the porch to meet us, and grabbed my hand. "Don't be shocked, Renee," she whispered. But as I tip-toed behind Ruth into the thickly-carpeted room, I recoiled in anguish at the sight of the brown, metal coffin at the front. It looked so cold. *How could my brother be in there?* I edged closer to the row of chairs lined before it and sat down in the front beside Ruth and my parents. For several minutes none of us spoke as we stared at the coffin. I glanced at Mom to see her mouth quivering and eyes moist. Dad, seated next to her, also looked grim, not saying a word. Finally, several of us broke the silence and prayed out loud in succession. Then Dad opened his Bible and started to read.

"You believe in God. Believe also in me. In my Father's house are many mansions . . . ." Dad's smooth voice continued over the beloved phrases, like the smell of the flowers in the room. Ruth, then, began to read another familiar verse. As we continued sharing scripture and singing songs of worship, the pain began to lighten.

Only later did I learn how Ruth herself faced the shock of that coffin—she had spent an hour alone with Dana, as soon as the funeral director prepared him. She recorded her heart's cry in the following words:

> *Here I sit before the casket of my husband. Father, what mystery in death—such grief and despair, yet such hope and victory. I can't believe Dana is in there. I want to open the coffin just to make sure. In some respects I wish he had been found earlier as I find it dissatisfying almost that I cannot see him one last time. But Thou hast ordained this day for me before it existed and I trust in Thee for the timing.*
>
> *I thank You for this time to worship. I feel as Abraham must have felt when You asked him to sacrifice Isaac, his only son. He obeyed You and went up the mountain to worship.*
>
> *Just because, God, You chose me to truly sacrifice what I held dearest to me, does that*

> *mean I should not climb the mountain to worship? Unlike Abraham and Isaac, God, this time You chose the sacrifice to be complete. I joyfully worship You with the attitude of Abraham of old. This is my opportunity to worship and honor You.*

Ruth later shared with me afterwards that as she began to worship, a blanket of peace descended over her. She knew absolutely that Dana's "true self," his spirit, wasn't in that box—and the coffin wasn't as important anymore.

By the time we left, 30 minutes later, I was feeling a little better. I could face the graveside service tomorrow. In fact, I felt so much better I decided to prepare a short message to give at the service and sing a familiar duet with my father.

The next morning, however, my courage failed as I stood on the grass of the small, fenced-in cemetery, viewing the mound of fresh dirt overturned for Dana's grave. As my eyes fell on the beautiful marker that Ruth had told us about, my knees grew weak under the August heat. There was the cross and the dove, just as she had described. But then I read the dates: 1958-1984. 1984—it was so final. The end.

Vainly, I tried to grasp some comfort from the scripture verse etched on the stone. "And this is eternal life, that they may know Thee, the only true God, and Jesus Christ whom Thou hast sent" (John 17:3 NAS).

When a small crowd of mostly elderly people began to gather, a black hearse pulled up nearby and my despair deepened. My heart sank to my stomach as I observed my dad, erect and composed, helping to carry the coffin with three other men. They lowered it over the grave, next to Madonna Gail's, and although Dad's face was outwardly calm, I was worried. Dad had shared with me earlier that he didn't know if he could go through with our duet. Music affected his emotions so deeply. But then my grandparents' minister took his place beside the coffin to begin, and the moment to change plans had passed.

The serious young preacher began the service by leading the 50 of us gathered at the graveside in the hymn, "Holy, Holy, Holy." A lump mounted in my throat and my eyes stung. *How could I possibly sing a duet?* Then I looked at Mom standing beside me, tall and straight, with her head held high. Her brave soprano rang out despite her sorrow and it gave me a little hope. Feebly, I lifted my shoulders and prayed. *Give me courage to survive this!* I begged.

Ruth stepped forward, a small, bold figure, fresh and attractive in a purple dress. She shared a message based on John 17:3, the scripture engraved on Dana's marker and a favorite verse of Dana's. She explained to our group what eternal life was and how one could receive it by faith in Jesus.

But soon my mind wandered, jumping ahead to what was next. Dad and I were supposed to sing as soon as Ruth finished!

What happened next was another little miracle— seemingly unimportant until seen later, and added up with others. As I took a deep breath and one step toward the coffin, my feet felt light and I literally wanted to skip! I couldn't believe it! A strength that I hadn't known before began to lift me from my sorrow.

Radiantly and from my heart, I explained to the small crowd that if Dana could now address us from his vantage point in heaven, he might quote a favorite passage from Jim Elliot's book:

> I'm in heaven now. It is exalting, delicious.
> The heavens are hailing my heart. Oh, to
> gaze and glory and give oneself totally to
> God; what more could I ask? Oh, the full-
> ness, pleasure, sheer excitement of know-
> ing and being with God. On earth all I
> wanted was to love and please Him and
> now—now I can finally see Him, touch His

garments and smile into my Lover's eyes.
Oh, nothing on earth matters or compares
to knowing, seeing and being with Him for
all eternity.[6]

Out in that country cemetery, surrounded by the plains of Montana and far off mountains, I continued. I told those gathered what I thought God could have said to Dana and to every believer whom He greets in heaven: "You have fought the good fight, you have finished the race, you have kept the faith. Henceforth I will give you the crown of righteousness, which I, the righteous judge, will award to you, and not only to you, but also to all who have loved my appearing" (II Timothy 4:7-8).

As I finished speaking, standing beside the coffin, my father came forward and joined me, smiling. His hazel eyes radiated peace and I felt God was giving him the strength he needed too. Together we raised our voices exultantly in a song by Keith Green, a Christian singer who died in a plane crash shortly after recording it. As our voices harmonized to the tune of "There Is A Redeemer," we sang it as Dana could have been singing on this, his one-month anniversary in heaven:

I'm with my Redeemer,
Jesus, God's own Son,
Precious Lamb of God,
Messiah, Holy One.

Here I stand in Glory,
I can see His face,
Now I can serve my King forever
In this Holy Place.

Thank you, oh my Father
For giving me Your Son,
Now I can serve You here forever
Since my work on earth is done.[7]

As the service ended, several people came forward to

shake our hands, expressing surprise over our family's strength and participation in the service. I was so grateful to God. I was learning to experience a joy that wasn't based on the absence of suffering, but a joy found only in His presence.

I climbed into the back seat of the small car with Ruth beside me and my parents in front. As Dad started the engine and began to pull away, suddenly I turned to search out that brown, metal coffin. Fastening my eyes on it as we drove on, I watched as it became a small brown dot, finally disappearing out of sight.

Swallowing hard for a moment, I tried to remind myself that Dana was not really there, only the "house" he once lived in. Dana was now in a better place altogether. Then I lifted my eyes to the regal mountains of Glacier National Park rising in front of me, remembering God's faithfulness to us that morning. With newfound hope I could readily agree that, "The steadfast love of the Lord never ceases, his mercies never come to an end; they are new every morning; great is thy faithfulness" (Lamentations 3:22-23).

After a full day of meeting people in my grandparents' home, I lay beside Ruth in the bedroom, exhausted from the service. But as I drifted off, all of a sudden I heard the front door come crashing open in the living room, jolting me awake.

Ruth pulled herself up in bed, wide-eyed with confusion.

"It's just the wind. A thunderstorm, Ruth," I explained nervously, trying to calm us both. But I was too frightened to venture out to close the door myself. "Would you mind closing it, Ruth?" I asked sheepishly.

Eyes full of sleep, Ruth nodded and shuffled toward the living room. I looked out the window just as the sky split open with lightning and loud crackling thunder, and crept under the covers as I waited for her to return.

When Ruth came back a few minutes later, her face was crumpled in despair as she climbed back into bed.

"I feel so lonely, Renee. My first Montana thunderstorm and Dana's not even with me."

I nodded understandingly. Dana loved thunderstorms, and now Ruth was experiencing her first one in Montana on the very night of her husband's burial. What it would have meant if she could share that moment with him.

As Ruth lay down beside me, I knew more than ever that somehow God would have to help her. We were in the midst of a storm that came bolting down as a result of Dana's death—and we'd only find refuge nestling in the center of His will.

The four of us, my parents, Ruth and I, all headed back the next day on the long trip home to California. The trip wasn't made any easier by our own private battles with loneliness, sorrow, despair and even the stubborn desire to deny what had happened.

The little things kept the pain intense. Driving Ruth's and Dana's small car, we stopped to eat in Idaho Falls. Returning to the car from the restaurant, Ruth stared at our rear bumper. I looked to see a remnant of string hanging down. Then I remembered—it was left from their wedding, once holding a joyous clatter of cans.

Cycles of tears, loneliness, sorrow, anger, denial, apathy, and questioning were all part of the grieving process we were living. Jesus wept when his friend Lazarus died, and this was our time to sorrow also.

But God had also been clearly showing me our need to accept His acts of love. If we refused to be comforted, immersing ourselves in self-pity, anger or an unwillingness to move forward through the grief process, it was actually an act of unbelief. Gradually we were learning to accept God's help and move on.

But the healing process was still much slower than any of us could have guessed. And a few days later, as we pulled into the driveway of my parents' California home, we would begin to see how many more tears were yet to come. Through it all, our trust, hope and faith in God would go through difficult tests when our feelings overshadowed His truths. We often failed, but God never did. All along, I knew He was there, patiently waiting to comfort, listen and pour out His grace on me and my family. But in my all-consuming sorrow, I didn't always feel like reaching out to God, or even trying to be in His presence during those dark despairing hours.

PART IV

LEARNING TO WALK AGAIN

"For to this you have been called, because Christ also suffered for you, leaving you an example, that you should follow in his steps" (I Peter 2:21).

Riding the Roller Coaster

The front door opened and my mother appeared, hunched-over with the color drained from her face. She had just started back to work in the fall as a secretary at a nearby high school, and all of us felt growing concern for her. Dad and Marty had poured themselves into their consulting work, finding therapy in keeping their minds challenged, but with Mom it was different. In her tired and grief-stricken state, she had no reserve left to cope with a co-worker's unkind word or a boss's insensitivity. It took great effort for her to put on the expected smile of bravery. By the time she came home each evening, Mom was exhausted from the combined struggle of doing her job and keeping her feelings under control.

I too was feeling the strain of Dana's death and had decided not to teach again that fall. Instead, I tried to keep busy at home, cleaning and running errands, until I could make a decision about my future. But all too often, I spent my days surrounded by Dana's pictures or other belongings I would come across. Opening a closet or pulling out a drawer, there would be Dana's clothes or camping gear. But what should have been cherished mementos brought also a keen awareness of Dana's absence. Part of me longed to linger over Dana's pictures and hold his belongings, yet I also drew back from them and the overwhelming sadness they brought. Gradually my pain lessened but my emotions still felt brutally battered.

One day Mom arrived home from work looking especially edgy and tired. She slumped down in the recliner next to me and began to go through a long familiar list of *if onlys*. As she ticked off each item, I listened patiently.

"If only they didn't go on that trip...."

"If only they'd never joined that Bible study group...."

"Why did that group have to go to Canada, anyway?"

I didn't know how to answer. It didn't help that no one in the Bible study group had visited us since their return from Canada and Alaska. Maybe they were afraid to come over, not knowing what to say? But Mom couldn't see that in her grief and anger. And we never knew to expect unreasoning anger as part of mourning.

"What I especially don't understand," Mom continued, her ire rising, "is how your dad and brother can be so loyal to that group! They haven't missed a meeting since we got back." Tears of anguish spilled out of her blue eyes as I groped for something to say.

Angrily she wailed, "If only they hadn't started the Bible study in the first place, they would have never known about that stupid trip!" Finally I had to say something.

"Mom," I started slowly, "you're going to have to believe that God loves Dana more than you do. He could have prevented it from happening."

Jolting out of the recliner, my mom stormed out the front door and slammed it behind her. Obviously, I had not helped her at all, but only made it worse.

Unsure what to do, I slumped in my chair and watched TV, waiting for her to come back.

I could never have predicted what happened next. After 30 long minutes, the front door opened and in sauntered my mother with dry eyes and a relaxed face. *What happened?* I watched in surprise as she headed for the kitchen and heard her singing softly as she washed the dishes.

I sat in the living room, trying to take in what it meant.

At last I saw that Mom's questioning and subsequent anger had run their course, and no amount of coaxing or rational arguing had made any difference. It was clear that what a grieving person needed most is an understanding ear, and to save the theology for later.

Grief was like a roller coaster we were riding, and over the next few weeks we experienced many more ups and downs. Sadness, depression and apathy would take us down hard for a day or two, only to be followed by upward swings and relief to our fluttering stomachs and shell-shocked emotions. Ignoring, resisting, or trying to deny our grief only seemed to cause our emotions to spring up later with greater fierceness. We did our best to keep short accounts with our emotions and deal with them honestly as they came. Otherwise, we found we paid our dues later with added interest.

Not that we gave in to our emotions entirely. We didn't want to be at the mercy of our "gut-level feelings" and languish in self-pity, bitterness, anger or depression. We had already discovered some powerful weapons against these if we would be willing to use them. One was to be thankful for God's faithfulness, love and grace. If we focused our eyes on Him, taking them off ourselves, it was a sure antidote for self-pity.

Reading the Word of God often helped get our emotions in line with His truths and gave us His fresh perspective on our loss. The temptation to be angry at God diminished as we read throughout the Bible of His tremendous love, compassion and unfailing mercy.

And lastly, we learned to become like little children before our heavenly Father, helpless and dependent before Him. This enabled us to receive His very real and sufficient comfort.

On August 27th, we held a small celebration for my parents' 32nd wedding anniversary. A few close friends gathered around my family in our dining room as I began cutting the angel food cake. Placing two pieces in front of Marty and his wife, Rosie, I glanced at my tall, curly-haired brother. Just a few days ago they had surprised us with the news that Rosie was pregnant with their third child. I knew Marty was excited over this unexpected news, but for some reason, he appeared untypically quiet and withdrawn this evening.

Earlier that evening, Rosie told me Marty had finally been confronted with the reality of losing his only brother. As they had watched a movie one evening about a football player dying of cancer, Marty became strangely subdued when he learned the man had been just 26—the same age as Dana had been. Rosie explained that after the picture ended and they got into bed for the night, she heard a loud sniffle from her husband. Suddenly Marty blurted, "Sometimes the reality hits me, and it's hard!" Putting his face into his pillow, he just sobbed.

After several minutes, Rosie encouraged him to cry and express the loss he was feeling. Finally Marty began to talk and it all came out in a stream. He and Dana had always gotten excited about the same things, whether it was a spider or a piece of machinery—and now a part of him was gone. How Marty missed that. "He was the only brother I had," Marty whimpered over and over.

But as Rosie told me the story, I knew it was a new step. Marty was beginning to open up now and let God heal his wounds.

I continued passing out pieces of cake, and as I gave the last one to Ruth, I realized she was undergoing a far different battle. Several days ago, she shared with me how Dana sometimes walked out on her during a disagreement. But before he died, Dana promised he would never do it again. Now he had done the ultimate and walked out on Ruth for good!

Feelings of being deserted seemed inescapable to Ruth. She even dreamed she saw Dana again, but then he left her, going back to heaven. Ruth confided she knew of cases where people had seemingly died, and the Lord allowed them to choose to live again. What if Dana had actually been given the option to return, yet decided to remain in heaven without her? She was plagued with the worry that perhaps Dana didn't care about the pain she was going through as a result.

As Ruth admitted these feelings of rejection and insecurity, she told me she had had to make a deliberate choice to trust both Dana and God. As she did so, truly putting her feelings in God's hands, the rejection and desertion lifted.

Now I watched as Mom began to open their anniversary gifts, the first one being from Ruth. Mom smiled sweetly at her as she held up a framed picture of a house which Ruth had embroidered. Dad, seated next to Mom, read the caption out loud: "In my Father's house are many mansions" (John 14:2 KJV).

Mom opened my present next, a short poem I had written as though Dana were writing to my parents. I listed three men Dana would be enjoying heaven with: James and John, the apostles, and Jim Elliot. Framed with the poem was Dana's picture, taken for his residency just a week before his death.

Now my mother read my poem quietly to herself as Dad looked over her shoulder. Soon teardrops began to escape from Mom's eyes, and she handed it to me to read to everyone:

> I'm here in heaven now
> With James and John and Jim,
> As Jesus is instructing us
> To rule and reign with Him.
>
> Although I can't be with you
> On your anniversary,
> We'll have a grand reunion soon
> For all eternity.
>
> You've invested me in heaven
> So don't sorrow or be sad,
> Just remember 'til we meet again,
> I love you, Mom and Dad.

As the poem was passed around the table, I tried to take consolation in the fact that one day we'd be reunited with Dana forever in heaven. But deep down, I still wished Dana were here right now with us.

During the next few weeks, Ruth still struggled occasionally with dreams and feelings of rejection over Dana's death. What would help her in the battle? A friend encouraged Ruth to meet with her pastor's wife, whom she thought might help, and Ruth hesitantly agreed.

Coming home from meeting with the pastor's wife after a Sunday evening service, Ruth sat down with me at the kitchen table to tell me what happened.

"She asked me to imagine holding Dana's hand," Ruth explained. "And then she asked if I was willing to let go."

"And were you?"

"Oh, yes. Then she said Jesus was coming to take Dana's hand and asked if I would let Him."

"And?"

"I said yes again," Ruth went on matter-of-factly. "Then she had me picture Jesus taking Dana away and Dana waving goodbye to me. Still I felt fine, but then . . . ."

Ruth's voice trailed off and she remained silent for several moments as if reliving what happened next. Slowly Ruth began again. "She asked me to see Jesus letting go of Dana's hand and reaching out to take mine. I . . . I didn't want to take it."

I just stared at her in surprise. If Ruth could let go of her husband's hand, say goodbye to him and let Jesus take him away, why couldn't she bring herself to take Jesus' hand? Ruth looked away.

"I . . . I found it was Jesus Himself I couldn't trust."

I sat there, quiet, afraid to say a word. Ruth had to get through this.

"I was afraid to take Jesus' hand," Ruth began again. Afraid of the pain. Afraid of the future."

I nodded, understanding. She had lost her sister and two nephews, went through her parent's divorce, and now her husband had been taken as well. The hurt of it all was so great. No wonder she was afraid to reach out in trust again, fearing even greater sorrow.

The revelation was new to Ruth. Now that she saw her problem was a lack of trust, she deeply desired to overcome it. Over the next few days, I watched as Ruth, through a bare act of her will, began to speak out her trust in God and His character. She told me how she chose to believe Bible verses such as, "The Lord is near to the brokenhearted, And saves the crushed in spirit" (Psalm 34:18) and ". . . the Lord longs to be gracious to you, And therefore He waits on high to have compassion on you. For the Lord is a God of justice" (Isaiah 30:18 NAS). She then began to imagine a picture of herself taking Jesus' hand, remembering such verses as " . . . Thy right hand upholds me" (Psalm 18:35 NAS) and "The steps of a man are established by the Lord; And He delights in his way. When he falls, he shall not be hurled headlong; Because the Lord is the One who holds his hand" (Psalm 37:23-24 NAS). Little by little, Ruth was beginning to trust God once again.

The Lord was also helping my mother walk through the valley. Mom told me of her vivid dream, unlike the previous nightmares about Dana. This time she saw her son walking up a hill holding onto a man's hand. Although she couldn't see the man's face, he wore a long white robe, and she knew in the dream it was Jesus. Dana's face glowed, and when Mom woke up, she felt a wonderful peace and comfort gently rock her back to sleep. For the next few days, Mom said she felt the same blanket of peace still settling upon her.

As Mom reflected on the dream, she realized Dana had a strong hold on the outstretched hand of Jesus. In the same way, for us all to survive in the valley, we too would need to walk with our hands firmly clasped in the Lord's.

The next month, Ruth received a special blessing— the opportunity to meet with Elisabeth Elliot—the woman whose writings, along with those of her slain husband's, had become such a guiding beacon for us all. As Ruth sipped tea and shared her story with this woman of God in her Massachusetts home, Elisabeth gave Ruth some simple but wise advice: "Be willing to do the next thing God tells you to do."

It sounded easy when Ruth shared it with me, but in a time of grief I often found I preferred to dwell on the past than to try to plan future goals. I felt listless and apathetic from so much grief.

But Elisabeth Elliot's words of simple advice grew in my mind over the coming days. I realized now how important it was to take the next step. I didn't want to get stuck, repeating the same stage of grief over and over again. Continued inactivity only seemed to result in more depression, impairing the healing process. Taking the next step I could, no matter how small, would be one step closer to ultimate recovery.

Like children first learning to walk, my family and I had often fallen down. But with practice we were slowly learning to stand up for longer periods of time, and eventually we'd be able to walk again without pain. *But what exactly was our next step?*

For Ruth, my mother and me, our next step soon became clear. Ruth and my mother would attend a Youth With A Mission Bible school and would be living in Sunland, California, located in the San Fernando Valley. I would be doing secretarial work nearby in Youth With A Mission's San Pedro office, while Ruth and Mom, along with 58 other students, learned about God's Word, His character, prayer, relationships and other biblical subjects. They felt being able to spend time apart growing closer to God would give them a renewed ability to face the challenges of life. Dad also was excited for them, and would drive down to spend the weekends with us over the next three months.

That September, Ruth and my mother left on their new step of faith—a step that would stretch them into new areas of growth and maturity.

I was glad I'd be nearby to see what happened.

Chapter 18
Learning and Growing

In September Mom and Ruth began their three-month Bible school training with Youth With A Mission (YWAM) in Sunland, California. Settling into a small trailer, along with several other women, they must have felt like real oddities at first. Ruth was the only widowed woman there and was even living with her mother-in-law. As I drove off, leaving them to face this new adventure, the Bible characters, Ruth and Naomi, stood out vividly in my mind. Even my sister-in-law's name was right: Ruth.

The new students, who were mostly in their early 20's, spent the first few days explaining why they were attending the school. Ruth later told me she shared the circumstances bringing my mother and her there, and the school leaders wanted to pray for them. As the students all gathered around, placing their hands on them in love and identification, the leader began to pray for God's blessing on them. My mother began to cry. She closed her eyes and was startled to see Dana standing along a beautiful pathway with golden wheat on both sides. His face glowed with contentment as he waved at her. Later she told me she opened her eyes and marveled over the vividness of the image.

When I visited them next weekend, Ruth and Mom

also reflected how greatly the touch of people's hands comforted them during the prayer. Those first months of loss had poignantly shown us how hugs, pats, and other physical contact were a real part of the healing process.

It didn't take long for the students to feel comfortable with Mom and Ruth after that, and for some reason, they refused the natural tendency to shy away from those in grief. Ruth and Mom's sorrow was greatly softened as they felt more and more at home there.

As the weeks progressed, I saw Ruth and Mom regularly on weekends. They told me how the leader's wife, Janet, befriended them in a special way, often inviting them to her room for coffee. Patiently, Janet listened to their struggles and often prayed for them.

I, too, lived in close proximity to others, working and living with 15 others at the Youth With A Mission office in San Pedro. Such community living forced all three of us to have positive contact with others, instead of following our tendency to socially withdraw. On the other hand, we also badly needed short times of withdrawal. Even Jesus went off by Himself when he heard His friend and cousin, John the Baptist, had been beheaded. During those times alone with God, I continually found I had to choose to look up and call on God with a direct act of my will. If I looked down at my grief, I was caught in a spiral of self-pity, loneliness and misery.

I shouldn't have been surprised—how many times had I read the words in my Bible, "Is any one among you suffering? Let him pray" (James 5:13). Yet now, in the aftermath of tragedy, the words seemed like they were written especially for our family.

Ruth also told me she liked to get away to the foothills near the YWAM school and pray. It energized her. Without it, she said her days dragged by. My mother, always an early riser, began getting up even earlier so she, too, could meet alone with God.

Jesus knew the vital importance of daily fellowship with God and often rose very early to meet with His

Father. Now, as we experienced the draining emotions and aspects of grief, it was more important than ever to spend adequate time in prayer, Bible reading and fellowship with God. For through it all, we saw it was God who could really comfort and give us the strength to go on.

And, slowly but surely, we were healing. There were times though, when I felt I would never recover from the wound that grief inflicted upon me. Once during a morning Bible study, the dedicated leader named Fay asked us all to mention another name for Jesus. Savior, Helper, Comforter, and Counselor were names people gave around the room. Then it was my turn. "He's our Redeemer," I offered. Fay nodded encouragingly.

"Well, that's like the lifeline principle," she responded.

"What do you mean?"

"Well," she began, "when a person is drowning, you throw out a lifeline to save him."

Drowning? Suddenly flashing before me was the dreadful sight of my brother, going under the water. *Why hadn't God thrown out a lifeline to save him?* My face melted in despair at her words and I quickly looked down before anyone could see my tears. Desperately, I struggled to control my emotions until the meeting ended.

Escaping to my room, I threw myself on the green quilt bedspread and began to sob. Why was I so touchy? Of course I was over-reacting! But telling myself that didn't help. Instead, waves of nausea swept over me as I huddled in a ball, crying out my sorrow and despair. My head began spinning as I searched for a way out of the fresh pain. I was sure Fay, a woman of faith and integrity, hadn't intended to hurt me, and certainly didn't know I was upset. Mustering my courage, I knew that I would have to tell her if I were ever to feel comfortable around her again.

Later that morning, as Fay opened the door of her home, she looked at my tear-stained face in puzzlement and invited me in.

"Renee, what's wrong?"

Brokenly I explained what happened. Fay nodded with understanding, and putting her arms around me, quietly prayed for that deeply sensitive area of my life. As her words ended, so did my tears. As I hugged her warmly and said goodbye, I knew a bruised area of my heart was now open to receive God's healing touch.

As Thanksgiving approached, it was hard for us as a family to face the holiday season without Dana. But again, God revealed keys to overcoming. As I was reading the Bible one day, these verses in Isaiah leapt off the page: "...if you pour yourself out for the hungry and satisfy the desire of the afflicted, then shall your light rise in the darkness and your gloom be as the noonday. And the Lord will guide you continually, and satisfy your desire with good things, and make your bones strong; and you shall be like a watered garden, like a spring of water, whose waters fail not" (Isaiah 58:10-11). These promises of guidance, strength, light and satisfaction all rested on one condition: giving and pouring yourself out on the behalf of other people. God was saying that to overcome my loneliness during the festive season, I needed to reach out to others perhaps in even greater trials.

Everywhere I looked in San Pedro I saw needy people. The YWAM center was located in a poor area of town, with plenty of street people milling nearby. What better way to celebrate Thanksgiving than to invite many of our poor and destitute neighbors to share a Thanksgiving feast with our community. Soon I was happily giving out invitations to people I came across—a young, unkempt woman longing for love and someone to listen to her sorrows; an old, feeble woman at a hospital for the retarded with no family or anyone who cared; and a strong, black man living in a beat-up car across the street. Together with my co-workers, we got busy preparing the meal, putting up decorations, and organizing a drama based on being grateful to God. It was amazing. The scripture verses God gave me were true! As I took my mind off myself, my own needs were taken care of.

Watching so many needy people enjoy a good meal that day, I remembered an ancient Chinese proverb about a woman whose only son had died. During her grief, she went to a holy man and asked if he could bring her son back to life.

After much thought, the holy man replied, "Find me a mustard seed from a home that has never known sorrow. We will use it to drive the sorrow out of your life."

Every place the woman went, people would describe all the tragedy that had befallen them. Finally the woman thought, *Who is better to help these unfortunate people than I, who have suffered so much, too?* So she stayed on in home after home, giving comfort and love to those in need until she became so busy helping others she forgot her own pain. Her sorrow was indeed, driven out of her life.

Later that Thanksgiving Day, my parents, Ruth and myself also gathered at my aunt and uncle's home nearby. As we enjoyed another turkey dinner, we saw how planning in advance for the holidays—being with people or doing some enjoyable activity—helped us overcome the loneliness and depression in our hearts.

As other difficult days approached—such as Christmas, Dana's birthday, and anniversary of his death, Mother's Day and Father's Day, I decided to plan some specific function and not be unprepared.

But the next big test was Christmas. And as the Bible school training ended, and we all moved back home for the season, we wondered. *How would we fare as we faced the sights and sounds of the most joyful holiday of all?*

Chapter 19

Setback

Memories of Dana greeted me at every turn. Beautiful, familiar Christmas songs were but cruel reminders of how Dana loved singing carols. And even tempting Christmas foods brought fresh memories of how Dana stood in our kitchen and made us all homemade fudge. Yes, Christmas was hard.

Then one day a letter arrived from Rhonda's husband. He had written to me occasionally in the months since her death, pouring out the grief in his heart. Often I'd gain new strength from his words, and new understanding in my own struggle. This letter was a real help:

> *Days seem to be filled with periods of a very subtle, chronic depression. During the day I yearn for quiet and peace. But coming home, the quiet sometimes turns to loneliness, and peace into a world that has apparently stopped. I know with the Lord's help I'll make it, but the weight of my life has become very heavy. I must constantly give my burdens to Him. When I fail to do this, my bag of burdens fills so that I can no longer carry it—only drag it along the ground. Oh, to*

someday give this bag up completely! Until
then, I will hand Him my burdens one by
one, hour by hour and minute by minute.

The letter couldn't have arrived at a better time. For
now, after five months of healing, new anguish was stirred
in my heart by the holidays. From Thanksgiving to New
Year's, our family had always celebrated in a big way.
Even Dad's birthday, December 10th, was part of the six-
week merriment. But now, it seemed we'd never be happy
again.

As usual, we gathered in Sunnyvale for Dad's birthday.
Although the small party was full of fun, memories of Dana
from past celebrations were ever with us. It might have
been harder for Mom than anyone. Later she let me read
these lines from her journal:

> *Going home was so painful this weekend.*
> *Trying to stay upbeat was rough. Dana's*
> *being gone seems harder with this Christmas*
> *season. I never dreamed the sadness that*
> *would be.*
>
> *Keith came home from church with tears in*
> *his eyes after singing, "Away In A Manger." I*
> *can't imagine ever being totally healed of*
> *this, but maybe the day will come when we*
> *will feel slightly mended—the rips sewn ever*
> *so gently. I loved that boy with every fiber in*
> *my body! I must refuse self-pity though, for I*
> *know that Dana would say, "Get on with it,*
> *Mom. There is much to do and learn."*

The season was a real setback for all of us—perhaps
the last big battle. Emotions we thought we had conquered
and overcome emerged and ignited once again.

With a vengeance, the anger came back for us all. For
Mom, it flared in what started as a very small matter. She

told me the story. She was worried because she was behind with her Christmas shopping. Then Dad asked her to take him to the airport for a short business trip.

Could my brother, Marty, take Dad instead? No, Dad had told her, Marty was to attend the Bible study that morning. My mother persisted. Couldn't Marty miss it just this once?

I stayed silent as Mom continued. I knew what was coming. All her old rage returned. Why had he and Marty stayed so loyal to that group of men who hadn't visibly supported us after Dana's death?

But my father still insisted Mom drive him to the airport, and her anger began to mount. By the time she got home, she was so upset that she furiously began to write down her feelings:

> *After what we've been through, how could my husband and Marty be so loyal? Not one has even come over to see us! Not one!! By the time Keith and I got to the airport, I was crying so hard I could hardly see. Rage, anger, or whatever, kept swelling within me. I started screaming. This went on all the way home until I had no voice. Was I losing my mind? Oh, God, let me die!!*

> *How could I come back from months of Christian training and a close walk with my Lord to feel such hate and rage? What was wrong?*

As hard as it was for me to understand the depth of Mom's feelings, I knew Jesus understood. He knew the pain mothers face when losing their children. His own mother, Mary, suffered from His death. Right after Jesus' birth, a righteous man from Jerusalem named Simeon said to Mary, " . . . a sword will pierce through your own soul also" (Luke 2:35).

Many years later, while Jesus suffered the agony of crucifixion, He was concerned for His mother's welfare. Even as He hung on the cross in horrible pain, he saw to it that His mother had someone to lean on. He gave her care over to the disciple He loved the most—John.

A sword had indeed pierced my mother's heart, and it would be many more months before her pain lessened enough for her to ultimately choose to forgive the group. In the meantime, her pain seemed too overwhelming for her to care.

At the same time, I knew Dad and Marty felt no disappointment toward the Bible study members because the group had never been close knit. Dad and Marty hadn't expected them to rush to our sides. But because of my mother's strong reaction, Dad finally decided to quit the Bible study completely, showing his greater concern for his wife's emotional well-being than his commitment to any group.

We found Christmas at my aunt and uncle's in Southern California far easier, away from all the old memories back home in Sunnyvale. And although Jody and Scott remained in Dallas, Jody wrote the following letter to encourage me:

> *Dear Renee,*
>
> *It's been a long, difficult year, but I sometimes think we need adversity to truly realize what friends, family and our Lord really mean to us.*
>
> *I'm sitting here listening to a song called "Home Where I Belong" (B.J. Thomas), and I remember how often Dana listened to it. Now he's really home with Rhonda and her son. And we're left to weep, but also to hope and to await the day when we're gloriously reunited!*
>
> *With love, Jody Lynn*

That Christmas the most cherished gift I received came from Ruth, a solid dove and cross charm like the one Dana had engraved on his wedding ring. Ruth also gave one to my mother, and my father bought her matching dove and cross earrings. Ruth even had a jeweler flatten Dana's ring itself and make it into a beautiful pendant she wore around her neck.

Somehow the shining dove and cross charm helped me remember too, what Christmas was really about, the story of God's incredible, unconditional love—a love so great it would allow His only Son to come down to earth, be born in a humble manger and eventually face the sort of suffering that few of us are ever called upon to endure.

Chapter 20

Mending

It was New Year's Eve as I sat in the Youth With A Mission center in San Pedro, listening to each one in the group tell what he or she could thank God for over the past year. But with each glowing report, I felt only loss. When my turn finally came, I tried to remain calm, but then the truth flew out of my mouth. "I just want to put a big X over 1984 and forget it ever happened!" I cried as tears forced themselves out of my eyes.

Sitting there on the beige couch with tears flowing freely, I felt so ashamed of my outburst. And although the others responded sympathetically after the meeting, I was sure they thought I should be "over it" by now. After all, Dana's death had been almost six months ago. So why wasn't I completely "over it"?

Later I found answers in the book *A Grief Observed,* by C. S. Lewis, telling about his grief after his wife's death. Lewis uses an illustration to relate why we don't easily recover:

> Getting over it so soon? But the words are ambiguous. To say the patient is getting over it after an operation for appendicitis is one thing; after he's had his leg off it is quite another. After that operation either the

wounded stump heals or the man dies. If it heals, the fierce, continuous pain will stop. Presently he'll get back his strength and be able to stump about on his wooden leg. He has "got over it." But he will probably have recurrent pains in the stump all his life, and perhaps pretty bad ones; and he will always be a one-legged man. There will be hardly any moment when he forgets it. Bathing, dressing, sitting down and getting up again, even lying in bed, will all be different. His whole way of life will be changed. All sorts of pleasures and activities that he once took for granted will have to be simply written off. Duties too. At present I am learning to get about on crutches. Perhaps I shall presently be given a wooden leg. But I shall never be a biped again.[8]

It was obvious my family and I were also still on crutches. But as I looked back, I could see how God was gently bringing us through each step—denial, questioning, anger, fear, apathy, loneliness and despair. But though we still limped along at times, we were making progress. And as we continued on our journey of grief, leaning on Him for guidance, strength and support, we would eventually take the step of acceptance—the final step toward restoration. Jesus is the one who walks before us on the road through grief and sorrow, and He is the one who has conquered death and reigns victorious.

Although we knew we would never be the same again, we could be grateful for being well on our way towards getting our wooden legs. And now that our stumps had had six months to heal, each scar that remained served only to remind us that we walked by the love, grace and power of our resurrected Lord.

Epilogue

It was Easter Sunday, 1985, nine months and three days after Dana's homegoing. Ruth, my parents and I sat in the morning church service singing hymns of Christ's resurrection. I had returned home with my mother to work as a secretary. Ruth now worked in a staff position for Youth With A Mission in Sunland. But little did any of us realize then, as Ruth sat serenely beside me, that three and a half years later one of her co-workers, a wonderful man named Mark, would become her future husband.

But today, tears easily came to our eyes, exhibiting our mixture of sorrow and joy—sorrow, from the deeply felt absence of Dana on this first Easter Sunday without him; and joy as we remembered the hope we have through the redemption and resurrection of our Lord. *Jesus has conquered death! Jesus has risen! Jesus reigns victorious!*

When we arrived home from church, we were made even more aware of God's tremendous faithfulness to us, seeing just how much He loves to bless, encourage and restore us. Just after noon that Easter Sunday, we greatly rejoiced to hear that Marty and Rosie had a new baby boy! And his name would be Dana.

Milestones to Recovery

1. *Give yourself time* to gradually adjust and accept your loss. Don't rush the realization. Go slowly when getting rid of your loved one's possessions, moving, or making arrangements that can wait.

2. *Do not put unrealistic expectations on yourself* by trying to go at the same pace that you normally do—grief saps your energy. But remember—prolonged inactivity can intensify your depression, preoccupy you with sad thoughts and impair the healing process. Therefore, do seek outlets.

3. *Put on the "garment of praise for the spirit of heaviness"* (Is. 61:3 KJV). As you focus your eyes on Him, you will find renewed strength and grace, and a sure antidote against self-pity.

4. *Spend time in prayer,* alone with God, telling Him how you feel. Come as a child before your heavenly Father, honest and open before Him, allowing Him to comfort you in your sorrow. Is any one among you suffering? Let him pray" (James 5:13) " . . . I will turn their mourning into joy, I will comfort them, and give them gladness for sorrow" (Jer. 31:13).

5. *Spend time in the Word of God.* It helps get our emotions in line with His truths and give us His fresh perspective on our loss. The temptation to be angry at God will diminish as we read throughout the Bible of His tremendous love, compassion and unfailing mercy.

6. *Reach out to others and don't withdraw.* Remember, "When sharing joy with a friend it is doubled. When sharing grief with a friend it is divided."

7. *Write down your feelings.* It helps release inner struggles of anger, remorse and questioning.

8. *Give out to others.* It will take your mind off yourself and will help overcome your loneliness. ". . . if you pour yourself out for the hungry and satisfy the desire of the afflicted, then shall your light rise in the darkness and your gloom be as the noonday. And the Lord will guide you continually, and satisfy your desire with good things, and make your bones strong; and you shall be like a watered garden, like a spring of water, whose waters fail not" (Isaiah 58: 10-11).

9. *Prepare in advance for the holidays or other days that may be difficult*—Mother's and Father's Day, the anniversary of his death, birthday, etc.—to be with others or find some activity you enjoy.

10. *Keep short accounts with your emotions* and deal honestly with them; otherwise they'll spring up later with greater intensity.

11. *Be willing to take the next step,* refusing to immerse yourself in self-pity, anger, depression or an unwillingness to be comforted. Otherwise, you can get stuck in repeating the same stages of grief over and over again. " 'For I know the plans I have for you,'

declares the Lord, 'plans for welfare and not for calamity to give you a future and a hope' " (Jer. 29:11).

12. *Remember God's acts on your behalf* and write them down. Here is a little list of God's mini-miracles to our family:

- He prepared Ruth for the loss of her husband through reading the story of Elisabeth Elliot's journey along the same path.

- He gave my father an unshakable faith and peace right after the accident.

- He sent another widow Ruth's way when she needed someone to identify with in Tulsa.

- He gave my mother peaceful nights again.

- I experienced joy out of nowhere in my hotel room on my way to Montana.

- He gave Ruth an overwhelming peace when she spent time before the coffin and a deep knowing that Dana wasn't there but with Him.

- I found a joy not based on the absence of suffering, but in the presence of God while speaking at Dana's graveside.

- My Dad was able to sing at Dana's funeral with me; an indescribable peace had settled upon him.

- Ruth was able to meet with Elisabeth Elliot in her home which was such an encouragement to her.

- God clearly prepared the next step for Ruth and my mother to attend the Youth With A Mission school in southern California, which provided these opportunities for healing:

    – My mother saw a vivid picture of Dana in heaven while the others there prayed with her.

    – The leaders' and students' love, acceptance and support—their hugs, willingness to listen and reach out to them were a great comfort, easing their sorrow tremendously.

    – The different Bible teachings each week on God's wonderful attributes of faithfulness, love, mercy and grace helped give them fresh new perspective in their grief.

- On Easter Sunday, nine months later, God gave us a new life in our family—and we named him Dana.

- On September 3, 1988, Ruth married Mark Custance, a Canadian who shares her love for God, and has a heart for overseas missionary work, to which they feel called.

NOTES

1. Elisabeth Elliot, *Shadow of the Almighty* (San Francisco, CA: Harper & Row, 1958), p. 43.

2. Elisabeth Elliot, *The Journals of Jim Elliot* (Old Tappan, NJ: Fleming H. Revell Company, 1978), p. 356.

3. Elisabeth Elliot, S*hadow of the Almighty* (San Francisco, CA: Harper & Row, 1958), p. 89.

4. Horatio G. Spafford, *"It Is Well with My Soul."*

5. Elisabeth Elliot, *Shadow of the Almighty* (San Francisco, CA: Harper & Row, 1958), p. 13.

6. Elisabeth Elliot, *The Journals of Jim Elliot* (Old Tappan, NJ: Fleming H. Revell Company, 1978), p. 309.

7. Keith Green, Songs for the Shepherd, *"There Is A Redeemer"* (Port Chester, NY: Cherry Lane Music Publishing Co., Inc. 1982), p. 29.

8. C. S. Lewis, *A Grief Observed* (New York: The Seabury Press, 1961), p. 61-62.

You may purchase these books from the following distributors in your country:

USA
Frontline Communications
P.O. Box 55787
Seattle, Washington 98155
(206) 771-1153

AUSTRALIA
Christian Marketing
P.O. Box 154
North Geelong, VIC 3215
(052) 78-6100

CANADA
Scripture In Song
P.O. Box 550
Virgil, ONT LOS 1TO
(416) 468-4214

ENGLAND
Mannafest Books
Holmsted Manor, Staplefield Rd.
Cuckfield, W. Sussex RH17 5JF
(0444) 440229

GERMANY
Youth With A Mission
Military Ministries
Mozart Str. 15
8901 Augsburg — Stadtbergen
(0821) 522659

HOLLAND
Pelgrim Intl. Boekenckm
Rijnstraat 12
6811 EV Arnheim

HONG KONG
Jensco, Ltd.
G.P.P Box 1987
3-3113768

NEW ZEALAND
Concord Distributors, Ltd.
Private Bag
Havelock North
(070) 778-161

SOUTH AFRICA
Mannafest Media
Private Bag X0018
Delmas 2210
(0157) 3317

OTHER LIFE-CHANGING BOOKS
BY YOUTH WITH A MISSION AUTHORS

_____copy (copies) of **ANCHOR IN THE STORM,** Helen Applegate with Renee Taft. The gripping true story of how Helen and her husband, Ben, Captain of the mercy ship, the M/V Anastasis, persevere through insurmountable odds to hold on to their dream to serve God on the high seas. $5.95 = _____

_____copy (copies) of **ASIA: A CHRISTIAN PERSPECTIVE,** by Mary Ann Lind, a Ph.d in Asian history. A revealing survey for Christians with a heart for Asia. This book will serve as a basis for spying out the land, for intercession and for developing creative mission strategies. $7.95 = _____

_____copy (copies) of **BRINGIN' 'EM BACK ALIVE,** by Danny Lehmann, director of Youth With A Mission in Honolulu, Hawaii. Practical, bold, easy to read and use in teaching others how to win hearts to a loving God. $5.95 = _____

_____copy (copies) of **COUNSELING THE HOMOSEXUAL,** by Mike Saia, who has an active counseling and teaching ministry, and who has worked with YWAM in Holland, Germany and Sunland, California, where he presently lives. A sensitive, accurate and biblical manual for pastors, counsellors and families. $8.95 = _____

_____copy (copies) of **THE FATHER HEART OF GOD,** by Floyd McClung, Jr., Executive Director of YWAM. How to know God as a loving, caring Father and a healer of our hurts.
                                                      $4.95 = _____

_____copy (copies) of **FATHER, MAKE US ONE,** by Floyd McClung, Jr. Firsthand, personal illustrations on how you can experience the healing power of God's love and unity in the Body of Christ. $5.95 = _____

_____additional copy (copies) of **FLOWERS FROM THE BRIDGE — Milestones to Overcoming Grief.** $5.95 = _____

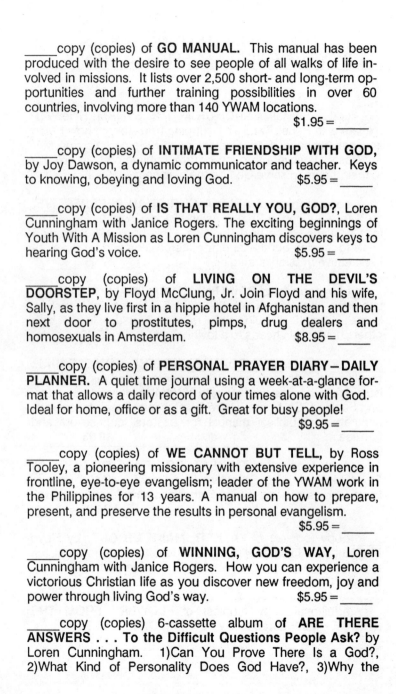

_____copy (copies) of **GO MANUAL.** This manual has been produced with the desire to see people of all walks of life involved in missions. It lists over 2,500 short- and long-term opportunities and further training possibilities in over 60 countries, involving more than 140 YWAM locations.

$1.95 = _____

_____copy (copies) of **INTIMATE FRIENDSHIP WITH GOD,** by Joy Dawson, a dynamic communicator and teacher. Keys to knowing, obeying and loving God. $5.95 = _____

_____copy (copies) of **IS THAT REALLY YOU, GOD?,** Loren Cunningham with Janice Rogers. The exciting beginnings of Youth With A Mission as Loren Cunningham discovers keys to hearing God's voice. $5.95 = _____

_____copy (copies) of **LIVING ON THE DEVIL'S DOORSTEP,** by Floyd McClung, Jr. Join Floyd and his wife, Sally, as they live first in a hippie hotel in Afghanistan and then next door to prostitutes, pimps, drug dealers and homosexuals in Amsterdam. $8.95 = _____

_____copy (copies) of **PERSONAL PRAYER DIARY – DAILY PLANNER.** A quiet time journal using a week-at-a-glance format that allows a daily record of your times alone with God. Ideal for home, office or as a gift. Great for busy people!

$9.95 = _____

_____copy (copies) of **WE CANNOT BUT TELL,** by Ross Tooley, a pioneering missionary with extensive experience in frontline, eye-to-eye evangelism; leader of the YWAM work in the Philippines for 13 years. A manual on how to prepare, present, and preserve the results in personal evangelism.

$5.95 = _____

_____copy (copies) of **WINNING, GOD'S WAY,** Loren Cunningham with Janice Rogers. How you can experience a victorious Christian life as you discover new freedom, joy and power through living God's way. $5.95 = _____

_____copy (copies) 6-cassette album of **ARE THERE ANSWERS . . . To the Difficult Questions People Ask?** by Loren Cunningham. 1)Can You Prove There Is a God?, 2)What Kind of Personality Does God Have?, 3)Why the

Cross?, 4)Creating With God, 5)Why War?, 6)How Can a God of Love Send a Man to Hell? $24.95 = _____

____copy (copies) of **LET'S TURN THE WORLD AROUND,** by Loren Cunningham. 1)Let's Turn the World Around, 2)Let's Go Barefoot, 3)Conditions For Knowing God's Voice, 4)Creating With God, 5)Go Means a Change of Location, 6)Releasing the Power of the Spirit. $24.95 = _____

$2.00 postage for 1-2 books/cassette albums plus .25 for each additional book.

QUANTITY DISCOUNT

4-9 items—10%
10-24 items—20%
25 items or more—42%
For Visa/MasterCard orders only call 1-800-922-2143

Number_____Expiration Date_____

Signature_____

ORDER NOW!

Send your order and payment to:

Frontline Communications – YWAM
P.O. Box 55787
Seattle, Washington 98155
(206) 771-1153

_____ Enclosed is $_____

Name

_____

Address

_____

City and State   Zip Code

_____(Check) For additional information on Youth With A Mission and a book/cassette catalogue.